PUFFIN BOOKS
Editor: Kaye Webb

Something to Do

Here at last is a book to fill up all the wet days and dull days that produce the question 'What can I do?' in every family. *Something to Do* has suggestions for things children can do at home, indoors and outside, without spending much money or being a terrible nuisance.

Each month has a separate chapter so that the games and ideas will fit with the proper season. February, for instance, that month of sniffles and chicken pox and measles, has a special section of Things to Do in Bed, and August, the holiday month, has a bunch of ideas to pass the time while travelling. Every month has its own special flower and bird to look for. There are tempting dishes to cook, things to make, games to play, and instructions for keeping pets.

This is every busy mother's *vade mecum*. It will refresh her memory on half-forgotten pastimes, and save her any amount of brain-searching with its detailed information and plans for practical entertainments.

Something to Do

By Septima

Illustrated by Shirley Hughes
Edited by Nancy Shepherdson
Diagrams by W. E. Bland

Penguin Books

Penguin Books Ltd, Harmondsworth,
Middlesex, England
Penguin Books Inc., 7110 Ambassador Road
Baltimore, Maryland 21207, U.S.A.
Penguin Books Australia Ltd, Ringwood,
Victoria, Australia

Published in Penguin Books 1966
Reprinted 1966, 1967, 1968, 1969 (twice), 1970 (twice), 1971 (twice)
Copyright © Septima Ltd, 1966

Made and Printed in Great Britain by
Cox & Wyman Ltd, London, Reading and Fakenham
Set in Monotype Bembo

Acknowledgement

We should like to acknowledge our debt to the
Oxford Junior Encyclopedia on which we have drawn
considerably for information about natural history

Contents

Introduction

We, the seven authors of this book, have twenty children between us aged between one and twelve. They do amuse themselves for a good part of each day, but very often their imaginations dry up and we are confronted with the plaintive question, 'What can we do now, Mummy?' As friends living in the same neighbourhood we found ourselves pooling our ideas, and this book is the result.

There are many people we would like to thank for helping us with it – our children, sisters, and cousins, not to mention aunts, uncles, and grandparents who have made and tested things, our daily helps who have cleaned up the mess, and our husbands who have endured it. But it is particularly dedicated to:

Carolyn, Clare, David, Hugh B.,
Hugh S.-S., Ian, Jane, Jeremy,
Judy, Julia B., Julia D., Kate,
Mark, Nigel, Olivia, Sarah, Simon,
Susan B., Susan D., and Toby

who helped us make it and we hope will still want to use it.

We also hope anyone who has ideas and suggestions for improving the next edition will write and tell us about them.

January

Winter Streams

Now the little rivers go
Muffled safely under snow,
And the winding meadow streams
Murmur in their wintry dreams,
While a tinkling music wells
Faintly from their icy bells . . .

Bliss Carman, 'Poems'
Dodd, Mead and Company, New York.

Twelfth Night

The word January comes from Janus, the name of the Roman god of beginnings, who was supposed to have two faces, one looking backward to the Old Year, and one forward to the New Year.

All over the world New Year's Day is gaily celebrated. People welcome it as the beginning of another year when all mistakes are wiped out and everyone can start afresh. It is the day to make New Year Resolutions.

In Scotland there is a New Year custom called 'first footing', when, at the last stroke of midnight on 31 December, people visit their friends to wish them a happy New Year. It is considered very lucky if your first visitor is a dark man, and even luckier if he brings with him a lump of coal.

On 6 January, the twelfth day after Christmas, we usually take down the Christmas decorations. It is called Twelfth Night and celebrates the coming of the Three Wise Men to see the Baby Jesus.

The Blue Tit

Tits are small birds with short bills, inhabiting most parts of the world. One of the most common tits in Britain is the blue tit. It has a blue crown (edged white), greenish back, wings and tail, yellow underparts, white cheeks, and a blue-black throat. It uses its bill to pick minute insects and grubs from buds or the bark of trees, often perching upside down.

It builds a beautiful cup-shaped nest of moss which is usually well hidden in holes in trees or walls. Towards the end of April it lays eight to eleven eggs, which are white, spotted with reddish brown.

The Snowdrop

Snowdrops flower in the middle of winter, thrusting up through the snow.

They are small, slender, solitary flowers with bell-shaped heads which hang downwards and give them a shy gentle look. They grow from a bulb, either wild or cultivated, in gardens, but look best in woods or groves where their white bells, edged palely with green and centred with yellow, and their fresh leaves, contrast brightly with the dark colours of the winter trees.

A Golden Hamster

Golden Hamsters are delightful little creatures and though they are livelier at night, are also alert and playful for periods during the day. They become very tame and can be allowed to run about on the floor. But beware! They have sharp teeth and can quickly eat their way into the furniture. They have been known to get out of wicker cages and disappear into sofas.

When you buy a hamster choose a young one with bright eyes. You will need a strong roomy cage, either of wood or wire, which can be kept indoors, as hamsters are clean animals and have no smell. Because hamsters catch cold easily they should be placed where there are no draughts. Line the cage with soft hay and put a handful of sawdust at one end. The hamster will make his nest and store his food in the hay, and you need only change it once a week. But the sawdust must be changed every day.

Buy your pet two small, solid bowls for his food and water. You can feed him at any time, as he keeps his food until he feels like eating it. His diet can be made from any left-over scraps, but should include meat, fish, cheese or eggs, and lettuce, cabbage or spinach, and, in winter, carrots, swedes or other root vegetables, and milk, which is very good for him. He needs a tablespoonful of solids and one or two of milk every day. Although he is very particular about his larder and doesn't like it disturbed, you must see that no mouldy food is left there.

Hamsters' lives are gay and short. They live only about two years. So, when he dies, remember him happily and choose another pet quickly.

Collector's Shelf

The New Year is a good time to start collecting all the odd-ments you will need during the rest of the year for making the things in this book.

Choose a safe place, a special shelf or drawer, to put all the things as you find them. Have a number of boxes, all ready and labelled for small objects – *corks, acorns* and *seeds, shells, drawing pins, paper clips* and so on. Or if you haven't room for lots of separate boxes use a large one and make divisions in it with strips of cardboard glued to the sides.

Use a large container for the *big* things you want to keep, such as pieces of cardboard, scraps of paper, cereal packets and egg boxes.

Make a list of all the things you want and pin it up on your collector's shelf and ask your family to help.

Once a week sort your collection and tidy your shelf otherwise it may become just a *junk* shelf.

As well as the things already mentioned you will find it useful to keep:

Picture postcards
Empty match-boxes
Illustrated magazines
Cotton reels
Plastic yogurt pots
Used matches
Scraps of wool and material
Pieces of lace and ribbon
Pieces of balsa wood
Strips of rubber and strips
    of linoleum
Scraps of carpet
Small nails and tacks

Pieces of wire
String
Sealing wax
Thin cardboard
Stiff board
Shoe boxes
Assorted boxes
Elastic bands
Pipe cleaners
Buttons
Gold and silver paper
Assorted tins
Insides of lavatory rolls

Ten Things to Remember
Every Month

1. Always put anything you are going to cut or pin on to a flat, firm surface.

2. Never work on a polished table, or on anything that can be spoiled, without putting newspaper down first.

3. Have a special pair of scissors for cutting paper and cardboard. If you use your sewing scissors they will be spoiled.

4. Put back tops on bottles. If you leave paste, glue or paint uncovered it will be no good next time you want to use it.

5. Always wash paint brushes when you have finished using them and clean any other tools you have used before putting them away.

6. Before starting work collect everything you will need so that you won't have to stop in the middle to look for something.

7. Make measurements very carefully and at once mark them neatly on your work so that you don't forget.

8. If you are doing anything messy protect your clothes with an apron.

9. If you are sewing be careful not to leave pins or needles lying about, and secure cottons and wools firmly after you have used them or they will unravel and become knotted.

10. When you stop work put everything tidily away and wash your hands.

Three Useful Things to Know

1. How to make a square

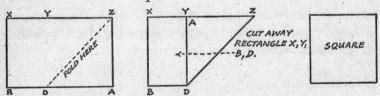

2. How to find the centre of a circle

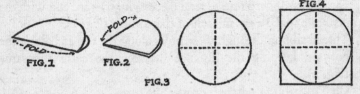

3. How to enlarge a drawing

Measure the drawing you want to make bigger at the widest part, both upwards and across. Then draw a rectangle of these dimensions and mark off every half inch all the way round. Then join your marks. See diagram. Copy the drawing, using the positions of the lines in the squares as your guide.

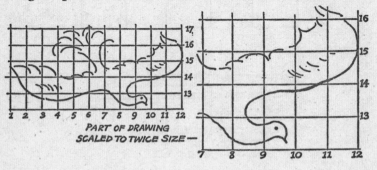

PART OF DRAWING SCALED TO TWICE SIZE —

Something to Make

What to do with Christmas Cards

Choose the largest and prettiest of the cards and keep them on your collector's shelf, clean and flat in a plastic bag. Here are some things you can do with them.

A Chinese Album

You need cardboard, or thick paper, ribbon, penknife, scissors, glue.

1. Cut the cardboard into several pieces 4 in. by 5 in. and with the penknife make a slit in each of the corners (Fig. 1).
2. Thread ribbon through these holes along the top and along the bottom, keeping the distance between the cards the same (Fig. 2).
3. Glue the ribbon where it crosses the cards.
4. Choose Christmas cards all the same shape, trim to the right size, glue one on to each of the prepared cards and allow to dry.
5. Turn over the whole string of cards and glue pictures on to the other sides. Allow to dry.
6. Fold up like a map. Trim the ribbon ends.

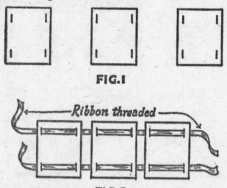

FIG. 1

Ribbon threaded

FIG. 2

Covering Notebooks – very easy

Choose a Christmas card the right size, and cut it to the shape of the book you want to cover, or cut out pictures from one or two cards. Paste the picture on to the centre of the notebook.

Holes punched for sewing

FIG.3

Sewing Cards

You need a pencil, darning needle, embroidery silk, or wool, or thin coloured string.

1. Choose a Christmas card without too much detail, such as a squirrel, robin, snowman or flower.
2. Mark the outline with pencil dots (see above).
3. Punch through these dots with a darning needle.
4. Thread the needle with the coloured thread, and sew up one hole and down the next, all the way round. Different colours can be used for different parts of the card. Neaten off the sewing at the back of the card.

If the Christmas card is on very thin paper, paste it on to cardboard before punching the holes.

Patchwork picture (or Box, or Screen)

You need cardboard, such as the lid of a dress box, scissors, glue, paper for 'frame', string.

1. Collect Christmas cards of all shapes and sizes.
2. Trim off the white edges.
3. Glue the cards on the cardboard, either working to a pattern or

at random, making sure that the cards fit closely to each other.

4. Stick a narrow edge of white or coloured paper round it for the frame.

5. Punch two holes at the top of the cardboard. Thread the string through the holes, and the picture is ready for hanging.

A patchwork Christmas-card screen is also very pretty and useful if you can find an old screen to stick the cards on to, or you can decorate a grocer's box with them and use it to keep your toys or your collections in. Keep very tiny pictures to use in your doll's house.

If you have lots of cards which you enjoy looking at you may find it interesting to sort them into subjects and make a scrapbook of them. On page 128 you will see how to make a scrapbook.

Making Railway Scenery

No train is much good unless it has somewhere interesting to go, and you can have a lot of fun making scenery to go beside the rails. But be sure to do this where it won't matter if you make a mess. You will need: old newspapers, a large piece of cardboard, a washing-up bowl, flour, water, green and brown poster paints, a large paint brush, pencil, old clothes to wear.

To Make a Hill

1. If your railway is fixed to a board, outline with a pencil where the hills and cuttings are to be. If it is not on a board, draw the shape of a hill on a large piece of cardboard, first making sure that it will fit inside the track, and then cut it out.

2. Crumple separate sheets of newspaper into balls.

3. Put several of these balls into the centre of the area you have marked for the hill, pushing them together into a hump (Fig. 1).

4. When the hill is high enough and the right shape, glue and stick the balls of paper on to the board and to each other. Leave to dry.

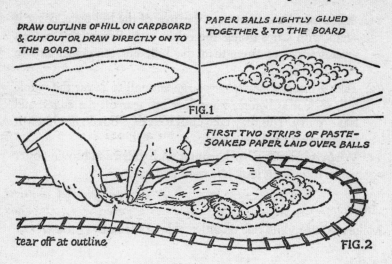

DRAW OUTLINE OF HILL ON CARDBOARD & CUT OUT OR DRAW DIRECTLY ON TO THE BOARD

PAPER BALLS LIGHTLY GLUED TOGETHER & TO THE BOARD

FIG.1

FIRST TWO STRIPS OF PASTE-SOAKED PAPER LAID OVER BALLS

tear off at outline

FIG.2

5. In the meantime put a few handfuls of flour into the bowl, slowly add some water, and mix into a smooth paste the thickness of cream.

6. Tear up some sheets of newspaper into strips about 2 ft long and 6 in. wide. When the glue on the paper balls is dry, put the first strip of newspaper into the paste, but do not crumple it. Make certain the strip is properly soaked, wipe off any surplus paste into the bowl and then gently lay the strip over the paper balls, smoothing it carefully into shape. Do not use any pressure when you do this, or the paper balls will collapse.

7. Smooth down the edges and tear off pieces which go over the pencilled outline.

8. Put another strip of newspaper into the paste, wipe off the surplus paste and lay it partly over the first strip and partly over the paper balls (Fig. 2).

9. Continue to add more strips of paper until the paper balls are completely covered.

10. If you find there are not enough paper balls at the edges of the hill, push some small ones underneath without gluing.

17

11. When you have been over the area of the hill once, cover it again with strips going the other way. Repeat this process several times to strengthen the hill, but remember not to press the paper.
12. Take a piece of newspaper large enough to cover the whole hill, soak it as before, smooth it on, tear off the edges, and leave to dry. This may take until next day, but do not hurry it or you may spoil the result.
13. When it is dry and hard, paint it with green and brown poster paints to make it look like grass and earth.

A Cutting

Make two steep hills one on either side of the railway track.

A Path

Put some glue on the hill in a wiggly line and sprinkle on a little sand. When it is dry brush off the surplus.

Fences

These can be made from matchsticks.

Telegraph Poles

Paint some small pieces of wire black and add balsa wood strips on the top.

Hedges

Make from sponge rubber cut jagged and painted green.

Trees

Buy some lichen from a model shop. Put thin wire into the lichen and then stick it into the hill.

Now imagine you are 6 in. high, and step into the middle of your newly made world.

Bags of Money

To start a mint* you will need thick white paper, thick brown paper, pennies, sixpences, shillings, crayons, paste, scissors. Use white paper for silver coins and brown paper for pennies.

1. Put a coin under the paper and rub a crayon lightly over it. Soon you will see the impression. Now, on a fresh piece of paper, do the other side of the coin.
2. Carefully cut out both sides of the paper coin and stick them together back to back.

This money is very useful for playing shops, or for learning to count.

Cotton-reel Windmill

You need two or more empty cotton-reels of different sizes, cardboard, cork, knife, nail, glue, scissors, egg-box.

1. Glue cotton-reels together, largest ones at the bottom.
2. Cut four sails from cardboard (Fig. 1).
3. Cut cup section from egg-box and glue it on top.
4. Cut a ring of cork about ⅛ in. thick and attach sails through this to top cotton-reel (Fig. 2).

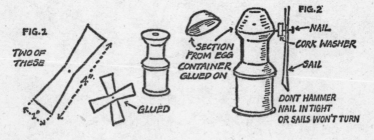

FIG. 2

TWO OF THESE

GLUED

SECTION FROM EGG CONTAINER GLUED ON

FIG. 2

NAIL

CORK WASHER

SAIL

DON'T HAMMER NAIL IN TIGHT OR SAILS WON'T TURN

* Mint: Place where money is made.

Learning to Knit

Here are instructions for casting on, plain knitting and casting off.

Casting On

1. Make a loop with the wool around the needle (Fig. 1).
2. Hold the needle in the right hand and the short end of the wool around the right little finger.
3. Wind the wool around the left index finger (Fig. 2). Hold the wool between the thumb and fourth finger of the right hand, put the needle in from below and slide the loop formed on to the needle (Fig. 3). Do not pull the loops too tight. Continue until you have enough stitches for the thing you plan to make.

Plain Knitting

1. Take the needle holding the stitches in your left hand and the empty needle in your right (Fig. 4).

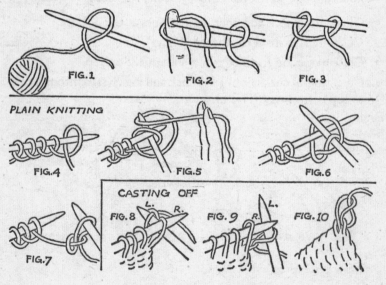

CASTING ON

FIG.1 FIG.2 FIG.3

PLAIN KNITTING

FIG.4 FIG.5 FIG.6

CASTING OFF

FIG.7 FIG.8 FIG.9 FIG.10

2. Place the right needle into the first stitch, and under the left needle.
3. Start with the wool on the right of the needle, take it round the point, and back over it from left to right (Fig. 5).
4. Draw the needle and wool towards you to form a new stitch on the right needle (Fig. 6) and slide the old loop off the left needle (Fig. 7). Continue to the end of the row.
5. Turn the work round so that the needle holding the stitches is again in your left hand and start the next row.

Casting Off

1. Knit two stitches on to the right needle. Take the right, or first stitch, over the left, or second stitch (Fig. 8) and slide it off the needle to the left (Fig. 9).
2. Knit one more stitch on to the right needle and repeat, taking the right over the left again.
3. Continue until you have only one stitch left. Break off the wool and bring the end up through the last loop. Pull tight (Fig. 10).

French Knitting

This makes a tube of knitting you can sew into a flat mat. Hammer nails into a cotton-reel and thread wool as in the diagram. Wind a circle of wool round the nails, then hook the first loops over to the inside. Carry on until the knitting is long enough, then break the wool, unhook the loops, thread the wool through, and finish off.

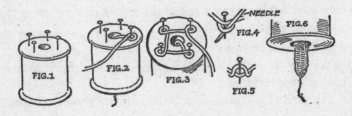

Three Games to Play

Boxes

You need a sheet of paper, two pencils, and two players.

Draw seven lines, one under the other, each line consisting of seven dots.

The object of the game is to form boxes. The first player draws a line, either horizontally or vertically, connecting any two dots he chooses, and the second player does likewise.

The players continue to take turns to join up dots. A player should be careful not to draw in the third side of any square if he can avoid it, as this will give his opponent the chance of drawing in the fourth and final line, thus completing a box. Each time a player completes a box he puts his initial in it, and has another turn. Thus he may well be able to complete several boxes in one turn. The winner is the one who completes the greatest number of boxes.

Up Jenkins

You need a sixpence, and any number of players.

This is a game for two teams sitting at opposite sides of a table. One team has a sixpence which it must conceal from the other, while obeying certain directions given by the leader of the opposing team.

Team A starts with a sixpence which is passed, beneath the table, from hand to hand, until one player keeps it, hidden in his hand. On the order 'Up Jenkins' from the leader of team B, team A place their hands on the table, firmly clenched. The leader of team B may now tell them to do any of the following three things:

Creepy Crawly – which means move fingers forward in a crawling movement.

Wibbly Wobbly – clenched hands must be turned over and back on the table, or

Flat on Table – hands must be laid down flat on the table.

Team B then guesses which member of team A has the coin. If they guess correctly it is their turn to conceal the sixpence. If they fail to guess, team A has another turn. The same player can keep the coin, or he can pass it on to another player when their hands are beneath the table again. The game continues in this way until the other team guesses correctly who has the sixpence.

Shadows

Hang a sheet across the room in front of a strong lamp. Turn off all other lights. Divide the players into two teams. Each team passes behind the sheet, one at a time, disguising their appearance as much as they can: by wobbling, wiggling, hunching their shoulders, sagging at the knees, staggering and lurching – while the second team must guess to whom each shadow belongs.

It is also amusing to act a play. But the story you choose must be very dramatic, as the audience sees only the shadows cast on the screen and the action takes place without speaking. For example, stage an operating scene in a hospital. Your instruments can be enormous ones cut out from cardboard; you will find their shadows look most alarming. Lay the patient out on a table near the sheet, pretend to cut him open and produce all kinds of strange objects from inside him, an alarm clock, a telephone directory, a football, a frying pan, and a tin of tomato soup.

Tea

Tea was grown in China and Japan thousands of years ago. Now it is also grown in India, Ceylon and Africa. It comes from a plant which, if it were allowed to grow freely, would develop into a small tree with flowers like a garden camellia. But it is pruned to make it grow into a bushy shrub.

When the leaves are green and tender they are picked by hand and dried. In China the freshly plucked leaves are withered on an iron pan over a wood fire, then rolled by hand and dried in the sun.

Once fast sailing ships called clippers raced from China to London carrying each new season's tea crops. Tea was so expensive then that it was kept in caddies with locks and keys. Now it is cheap enough for everyone to drink.

To Make Tea

Have ready the tea, the kettle and the teapot. The most important thing to remember is that the water must be boiling, so take great care not to spill any or you will scald yourself, and *always* put the tea in *first*.

1. Fill the kettle from the cold water tap and put it on the stove.
2. When it boils warm the teapot for a minute or two with a little of the hot water.
3. Drain the teapot and put in the tea. Take the pot to the kettle to fill, and not the kettle to the pot, as the water must be poured

boiling on to the tea leaves. One teaspoonful of tea for each person is the usual amount. Some people like it stronger than others, and some weaker, so you will have to experiment.

4. When it has stood for two or three minutes it is ready to pour out and drink.

Tea can be drunk either with milk and sugar, or with a slice of lemon. Lemon tea is very refreshing. China teas have delightful names such as Jasmin, Mandarin Leaf, and Lapsang Souchong.

Macaroons

You need 2 oz. ground almonds, 2 oz. caster sugar, 1 level dessertspoonful ground rice, 1 egg white, pinch of salt, pinch of cream of tartar, rice paper.

1. Grease a baking sheet and line with rice paper.
2. Put egg white, salt, and cream of tartar into a bowl and whisk until stiff.
3. Stir in sugar, ground almonds, and ground rice.
4. Place mixture in large teaspoonfuls on rice paper. If you like glacé cherries, place one in the centre of each macaroon.
5. Bake in oven at 300°, regulo mark 3, for about 30 minutes, or until the macaroons are golden brown.

How to Boil an Egg

If you would like to surprise your mother and father you could give them breakfast in bed. This can be done quite easily if you can make tea – see p. 18 – and boil an egg. All you need is:

A fresh egg

A small saucepan of boiling water.

Fill the saucepan with water and put it on the stove. When the water is boiling, place your egg on a tablespoon and lower it gently into the water, taking care that it does not crack. Put a bit of salt in the spoon too, to make sure. If you want the egg soft, boil it for 3½ to 4 minutes; if you want the yolk to be set firmly, leave it in the water for about five minutes. If it isn't going to be eaten at once, crack the top gently to stop it getting harder.

Enjoying the Snow

Tobogganing

For tobogganing you need wintry weather, snow, a slope and a sledge. Or, if you like, you can use a tray. But, for a smoother ride than a tray will give you, make this simple sledge.

The wood you use needn't be new, but can be old shelves, or broken-up packing cases, planed smooth and splinter free. You can also alter the measurements given, provided you keep them in the same proportions, to make a smaller or larger sledge.

You will need:

    2 pieces of wood 3 ft by 5 in., by 1 in. thick
    3 pieces of wood 16 in. by 6 in. by ¾ in. thick
    1 piece of wood 16 in. by 3 in. by ¾ in. thick
    16 screws, 2 in. long, no. 10 thickness
    7 ft of strip steel ¾ in. wide (steel 'strappings' off wooden packing cases may be suitable, but it can be bought)
    12 nails 1 in. long

1. Shape the two long pieces of wood to form 'runners' (Fig. 1).
2. Fit the other pieces of wood as the seat and footrest (Figs. 2 and 3). To fit the screws, it will be necessary to drill holes through the cross members, 'counter-sinking' these, so that the heads of the screws are below the surface; you may need someone's help to do this.

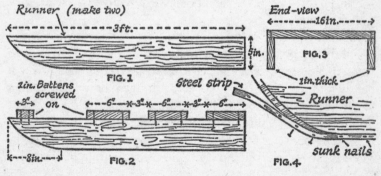

Runner (make two) — 3ft. — 5in. — FIG. 1
2in. Battens screwed on — 3" — 6" — 3" — 6" — 3" — 6" — 8in. — FIG. 2
Steel strip — End-view — 16in. — FIG. 3 — 1in. thick — Runner — sunk nails — FIG. 4

3. If you have managed to find some strip steel, nail this to the bottom of the runners, knocking the nail heads well in so that they are below the surface of the runner, as shown in the enlarged sketch (Fig. 4).
4. Whether or not you have been able to fit steel strips on the runners, the speed at which your sledge will travel will be improved if you rub the bottom of the runners with a candle or some beeswax.

Remember when sledging to see that no loose pieces of clothing or shoe laces are flying out which could catch in anything and spoil your run.

Eskimoes

Eskimoes live along the northern shores of North America and round the coasts of Greenland. In their country the temperature is rarely above freezing. In summer they build huts roofed with whale bones and turf, in winter they move out on to the ice floes and build themselves igloos. These are low domed houses made from blocks of frozen snow with transparent ice for windows. A skilled Eskimo takes less than three hours to build a snowhouse for his family. He covers the inside wall with skins and makes the bed from a shelf of packed snow.

Of course, the igloo is dark inside, so the Eskimoes have lamps made from soapstone. They use dried moss for a wick and the blubber of whale, walrus, or seal for the oil.

Eskimoes are great hunters and fishermen. They travel by water in small canoes called kayaks. Few edible plants grow in such a climate, so the Eskimoes eat mainly fish and meat.

Eskimoes are contented people, very good-natured and generous to visitors. They have enormous appetites and two

Eskimoes sitting down to dinner together can eat a whole raw seal.

They believe that if you scold a child his ears will grow too large, so they never punish their children, but pet them instead. The children grow up to be very kind and affectionate.

They have a very complicated language, and use one word where we would use a whole sentence.

IGDLORSSUALIORTUGSSARSIUMAVOQ is Eskimo for

He wants to find someone to build him a house.

To Make an Igloo

Wait until there is a good depth of crisp snow lying on the ground, then take a handful of it and pack it firmly together into a snowball. Go on covering it with more snow until it is too big to hold, then roll it about in the snow on the ground until it is about three feet high. Make two more snowballs the same size in the same way, then roll them all together.

Place a board on top of them and cover it with snow, packing the snow firmly so that all the edges are covered.

With a spade dig yourself an entrance. Put some straw on the floor, and a seat.

At night, pour water over the igloo so that the walls freeze hard and solid.

A Winter Picnic

Wait for the right day. One of those fine, clear, bright winter days, when everything looks and feels sharper than usual, and set off, very warmly wrapped up, to the nearest open space. This must be one where you can build a bonfire, where you can collect some wood for it, and, this is very important, where there is plenty of room for energetic games.

If the open space is near, you can walk there. But a picnic means lots of things to carry, so, if it is far away, you will have to go by bus or car or bike or train (by pony if you are very lucky), and take with you the food and drink and some dry sticks and paper to start the bonfire.

An insulated picnic bag is very useful if you have one. You can pack in it a hot meal – soup or stew, potatoes baked in their jackets, hot dogs, apple or mince pies – and it will stay hot until you eat it. If you have no such bag, then take food you can cook at the bonfire – potatoes, sausages, chestnuts, and a thermos of hot chocolate or blackcurrant juice.

As soon as you arrive at the place you have chosen, collect lots of wood and build a fire (see p. 142). Then, while it is getting hot enough to roast the potatoes and chestnuts, play a very warming game like 'He' or Leapfrog.

When you have eaten, it is time for more games. Let the youngest make first choice, or let each one choose in alphabetical order. But whichever way, choose quickly, for it is too cold to stand still.

Make sure not to leave any of your possessions behind. Be careful to put out the fire and clear up any mess.

Snowballs

You need snow!

First choose a Prisoner, who then goes away, leaving clear tracks in the snow. While the other players count a hundred, the Prisoner has to arm himself with as many snowballs as he can, and hide at some vantage point from where he can bombard his pursuers.

When the pursuers have counted slowly up to a hundred, they follow the Prisoner's tracks and try to capture him, whilst obeying these rules:

1. Each snowball thrown by the Prisoner which hits one of the pursuers scores a 'hit' and that player is out.
2. The Prisoner has won unless he is hit by as many snowballs as there are pursuers.
3. The last person to hit the Prisoner takes his place and the game starts all over again.

Christmas Roses, Spring Mint

In January the Christmas rose, whose proper name is Helleborus, will be flowering and winter aconites will also be in bloom. These are small yellow flowers with leaves grouped immediately beneath the head. They grow only about 6 in. tall and have tuber rootstocks.

This is the time to draw a detailed plan of your garden. You can colour in the paths, stepping stones, lawn and fence, and mark the sunny and shady spots. Then decide exactly what you wish to grow in different places and make a plan for sowing seeds in the Spring.

Early Mint

Dig up one or two roots of mint and, using ordinary garden soil, plant them in a flower-pot indoors. Make certain that there is enough drainage by covering the bottom of the pot with broken pieces of old pots or small stones, before filling with soil. Keep the plants in the light and well watered.

Indoor Gardens

If you happen to discover a large flat dish which no one else wants, use it to make a moss garden. Look in the woods for all kinds of mosses, which can be dug up in small clumps. To add colour to the moss garden dig up a primrose or violet root to plant in it, or conceal an egg-cup of water with winter flowers in it amongst the moss. Spray the mosses with water each week to see their colours and textures.

Care of Cactus Plants

During January give cactus plants a weekly drop of lukewarm water, to stop them shrivelling. Try to keep all your plants in as dry an atmosphere as possible, and away from any draughty window-sills.

February

Ha, Snow
upon the crags!
How slow
the winter lags!
Ha, little lamb upon the crags
How fearlessly you go.
Take care
up there,
You little woolly atom! On and on
He goes . . . 'tis steep . . . Hillo
My friend is gone!

T. E. Brown

Pancake Day

2 February is Candlemas Day, when the child Jesus was taken to Jerusalem to be presented to the priests, and Christians used to light candles for him and his mother Mary. In some parts of the country the snowdrops which appear in this month are called Candlemas bells, or Mary's tapers.

Shrove Tuesday (the forty-first day before Easter) was the day the early Christians went to confess their sins and be shriven. Nowadays we call it Pancake Day and eat pancakes as a feast before Lent comes.

This custom has its origin in the tenth century, when the Danes were invading England. In a part of Nottingham the men fled to the hills hoping the enemy would spare the women and children. But they took them into captivity and made them slaves. The women decided to rebel and kill their cruel masters, so they arranged to cook pancakes as a signal for the fight to begin.

Two ancient pancake customs still survive in England. There is a Pancake Scramble at Westminster School, when an enormous pancake is tossed over a bar in the roof of the great hall; the bigger boys scramble for it and the one who catches the largest piece wins a guinea. Also there is a pancake

race at Olney in Buckinghamshire which the women run, tossing a pancake as they go. Lent begins on Ash Wednesday, the day after Shrove Tuesday. This is the time when Christians remember how Jesus fasted in the wilderness for forty days, being tempted by the devil, and try to learn self control by giving up some of their favourite food or pleasures.

February is also the month when the famous Cruft's Dog Show is held, and when the skylarks and chaffinches begin to sing again. On 6 February 1952 Queen Elizabeth II came to the throne. The fourteenth of February is Valentine's Day, which is named after two early Italian saints. Birds are supposed to choose their mates on this day, and young men to single out their sweethearts by giving them flowers and sending them poems. There are only twenty-eight days in February, but every fourth year is a Leap Year, when it has twenty-nine.

B

The Great Tit

The great tit has a black crown and nape to its head, white cheeks and yellow underparts. The back is green, and the rump, tail and wing feathers are blue-grey with white outer tail feathers and wing bar.

From January to mid June you can usually hear his call: 'tee-cher tee-cher' (like an eager schoolboy). The nest is of grass lined with scraps, usually in a hole in a tree or wall. The eggs, laid in April or May, are white speckled with red.

February Flower

Lesser Celandine

Towards the end of the month you may be able to find some lesser celandine in flower, in damp sunny places by the road-side or on banks or in fields. They have leaves about an inch long and nearly as broad, rather like an ivy leaf. The flower rises singly from the root on a slender naked stalk. It is as broad as a shilling, of a shiny yellow, and looks like a star.

In olden days herbalists made a green cooling ointment of the leaves. The great celandine is about 3 ft high and its juice was once used for sore eyes.

A Cat

Kittens often come as presents, but if you buy one choose one which looks sturdy, and unless you have lots of time for grooming choose a short-haired one.

Keep a new cat indoors the first few days, and try putting butter on his paws to help him settle. His bed must be warm, soft, and away from draughts. To house-train your kitten either buy an earth tray and special crystals from a pet shop, or use a tray filled with fine ashes. He should be trained by the time he is a few weeks old, and will then soon adapt to going out.

A kitten is ready to leave his mother at the age of six weeks. At first the feeding rule should be 'little and often'. Meals can then be gradually reduced and the quantity increased until, at six months, he is having two a day. Give him fish, chopped liver (raw or cooked), milk, giblets, or meat. Tinned foods are all right occasionally, but not all the time. Remember to:

1. Remove all bones from food.
2. Take away the bowl after each meal.
3. Always leave some water down.

The commonest cat complaint is ear canker: always consult the vet about this. He will inoculate the kitten at six weeks against feline enteritis.

Playing in Bed

Because February seems to be the month when we catch most colds, or get all the infectious diseases, it seemed a good idea to suggest things you can do in bed. Of course, you don't *have* to be ill to do them. But it's a good thing to have a change from reading or colouring or listening to the radio. So here are some simple things to do which you may not yet have thought of:

A Handkerchief Mouse (to keep you company)

This little mouse is quite easy to make, and if you sit him on your hand and practise flicking up your fingers he will jump most realistically. To make him you need a large handkerchief.

1. Spread the handkerchief out flat and fold it in half so that corner B is on corner D (Figs. 1 and 2).
2. Fold corners A and C across each other (Fig. 3).
3. Turn it over so that the back is facing you (Fig. 4).
4. Roll up along the line, 1–2 (Fig. 5).
5. Fold D and B over the roll (Fig. 6).

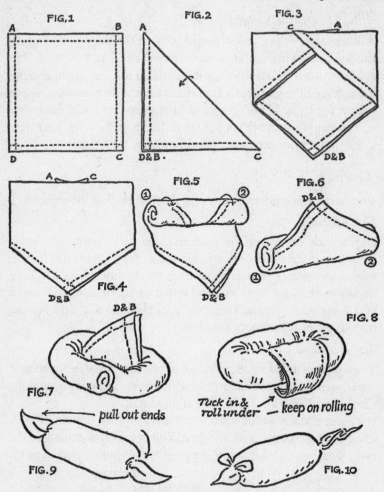

FIG.1 · FIG.2 · FIG.3 · FIG.4 · FIG.5 · FIG.6 · FIG.7 · FIG.8 · FIG.9 · FIG.10

6. Fold in 1 and 2 so that they overlap (Fig. 7).
7. Take D and B over 1 and 2 and roll inwards (Fig. 8).
8. Keep rolling until the corners A and C come out. If you have tucked them in too far you may have to pull them a little to get them out (Fig. 9).
9. Twist one corner to make the tail and tie a knot in the other to make the ears (Fig. 10).

The Umbrella Game

Ask someone to put an open umbrella on the floor near the bed, the handle sticking up. Then try to throw a ball into the umbrella. A heavy one is most suitable as it will often roll out again, and this is the fun of the game. If a friend can play with you, then he can collect the balls. Whoever gets it in twenty-five times first wins.

You can also throw rubber rings (from preserving jars) over small toys set out on a tray. (Good practice for the fair.)

Tracing

You need: tracing paper, soft pencil, 4 paper-clips, newspaper.

First Method

Fasten each corner of the tracing paper with paper-clips to a picture and trace the outlines. Turn the paper over, put it on a folded newspaper, and scribble over all the lines (Fig. 1). Turn tracing back to the right side and fasten on to the paper on which you want your picture. Draw over all the lines and then lift the tracing paper off without smudging.

Second Method

Trace picture as before. Scribble all over a separate sheet of tracing paper with lead pencil and place it between the tracing and the clean paper (Fig. 2). Trace over all the lines.

This method is useful when you want to trace a drawing beside another already on a sheet of paper. You can clip the tracing in the exact place you need it before slipping in the pencil-covered sheet.

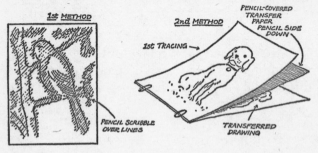

A Card Game – Roll Call

A good game for beginners. You need one pack, one player.

Turn the cards up, one by one, counting 'one, two', etc., up to King, as you go. Whenever the card turned up is the same as the number called it is thrown out.

When the pack is finished, start again with the remaining cards, without shuffling, and count on without a break. The player wins if all cards are thrown out, he loses if the cards being dealt keep coming up in the same order.

A Toy Lift

You need a *very* long piece of strong string, some cotton and three curtain-rings.

1. Put the long piece of string through the bar of the bed behind your head and secure loosely.
2. Thread the other end of the string round the rail at the end of the bed and slip the three curtain-rings on to it.
3. Holding on to the end, untie the string at the head of the bed and tie both ends together, making a belt of string that can be pulled round.
4. Tie a small aeroplane, or a little doll, or anything which might enjoy riding in space on to the middle ring with cotton. Tie the tail and nose of your aeroplane, or arms and legs of the doll, etc., to the other rings, leaving one long end of cotton. Then lie back and send your traveller off on his journey.

If your bed does not have a head and foot rail, ask someone to screw two largish hooks into the wall.

Pin People

You need paper and a pencil. Practise drawing these funny little men, and see how many actions you can make them do.

Mirror Writing

If you want to write a message to someone that you do not want other people to understand, such as 'come to the oak tree', write it backwards, like this: come to the oak tree When your friend receives the message, all he will have to do to read it easily is to hold it up to a mirror.

Before you can write backwards clearly you will need practice, and being in bed gives you a good chance to work at it.

Finger Shadows

With a clear wall and a bright light shining *behind* your hands you can make these, and invent others.

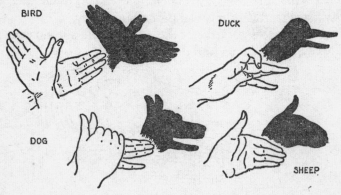

34

Marb   Bowls

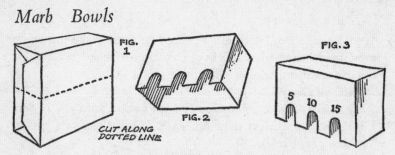

FIG. 1

FIG. 2

FIG. 3

5   10   15

CUT ALONG
DOTTED LINE

Cut a cereal packet in half and make arches in it (Fig. 3). Put it on
a tray, roll marbles down, and count your score.

Woolly Dolls

1. Cut a piece of card the width you want the doll's two arms and
   body. Wind wool round it twelve times, then slide it off and
   tie as in Fig. 1.
2. Cut a card the height you want your doll, wind the wool
   round twenty-four times and slide off. Tie twice near the top to
   make the head, then slip the arms through the body just below,
   and tie again (Fig. 2).
3. Cut the top loops for hair and sew on a face (Fig. 4).
4. If you want a girl doll, leave her as she is (Fig. 5).
5. To make a boy doll, tie the wool once more to lengthen the
   body, then divide and tie for legs (Fig. 3).

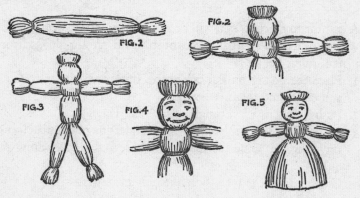

FIG.1

FIG.2

FIG.3

FIG.4

FIG.5

Writing a Diary

As you are in bed, with lots of time, you can make this more interesting than usual. You'll even have time to make pictures. Or you can make a special one like this:

My Mumps Diary

> *My name is . . . . . . I am . . . . . . years old. Until . . . . . . days ago I was as well as could be. Then I caught mumps (measles, chicken pox, a cold).*

and go on to put in all the things that happen to you, what you have to eat, the noises you hear outside, who comes to see you. You can draw the doctor and all your visitors, and yourself sitting up in bed.

Do it secretly, and when you are better give it as a surprise 'thank-you' to the person who took care of you. You can even write a *Dedication* like this:

> *For Mummy (or Auntie, or Nurse) – who helped me get better.*

A Match-box Cart

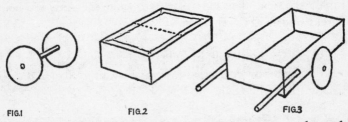

FIG.1   FIG.2   FIG.3

A cart for toy farms. You will need match-box tray, used matches with ends trimmed, small pieces of stiff card, strong glue, scissors, pencil, ruler, penny.

1. Place the penny on the cardboard, draw two circles round it and cut round them (wheels).
2. Push a matchstick through each circle (Fig. 1).
3. Mark a line along the centre of the underside of the match-box tray (Fig. 2). Glue the matchstick axle and wheels along the line.
4. Glue matchsticks for handles on either side (Fig. 3).

36

Paper Fortune-teller

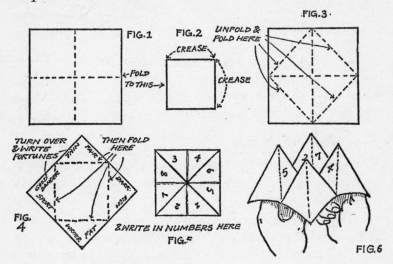

You need paper and pencil.

1. Take a square piece of paper. For paper square see p. 7.
2. Fold in half twice, corner to corner, and crease (Fig. 2).
3. Open, then crease the four corners into the centre (Fig. 3).
4. Turn over. Write fortunes round the edges (Fig. 4).
5. Turn these new four corners into the centre and crease.
6. Mark numbers on the flaps as in Fig. 5.
7. Fold in half. Open and fold in half the other way. Slip your two thumbs and two forefingers underneath the flaps facing you (Fig. 6). You will find that by moving your fingers and thumbs you open the 'pyramids' in two directions, one showing numbers 1–4, and the other showing numbers 5–8.

Ask your friend to choose a number between 1 and 4. If he chooses 3, open and shut the pyramids three times. Ask him to choose one of the numbers showing, and again open and shut the pyramids. Ask him a third time to choose a number, turn back the corresponding flap and read him his 'fortune'.

Three Minute Tent

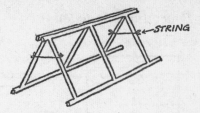

Make this hide-away place for games or secret plans. Use a clothes-horse tied with string with a rug over it.

Toy Shop or Theatre

You need a three-sided clothes-horse for this, also large sheets of paper, drawing-pins or sticky tape, scissors, paint or chalks, a piece of strong cardboard.

1. Stand the clothes-horse upright.
2. Pin or stick paper all over the clothes-horse, leaving the top half of the middle section open (Fig. 1). Decorate the walls if you have time.
3. Fix a cardboard shelf between the middle rungs of the two sides to make the counter or stage (Fig. 2).
4. A strip of paper showing the name of the shop, or theatre, can be pinned across the top.

If it is to be a shop, make some toy money (p. 13).
If it is a theatre you can make a glove puppet (p. 39).

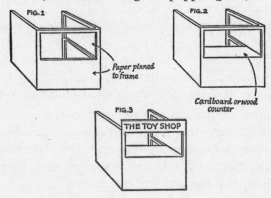

A Simple Glove Puppet

If you make this yourself, you can watch a friend grow as you work. You need the inside of a toilet roll, newspaper, material (coloured and white), scissors, needle, cotton, poster paints, ribbon.

1. Measure the length of your first finger against the cardboard roll, add about 1 in., and cut round the roll.
2. Crumple a sheet of newspaper into a small ball and place this in the centre of a folded single sheet of newspaper.

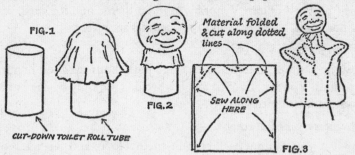

FIG. 1

FIG. 2

Material folded & cut along dotted lines

SEW ALONG HERE

CUT-DOWN TOILET ROLL TUBE

FIG. 3

3. Place the roll at the base of the ball, then fold the newspaper tightly round both ball and roll (Fig. 1).
4. Fasten by winding cotton round the roll and tying. Now you have the head and neck.
5. With a piece of white material cover the head, leaving a short length to go down the neck. Fasten with cotton.
6. Draw a face on the head. Colour with paints (Fig. 2).
7. Measure a piece of coloured material two and a half times the length of your hand and one and a half times the width of your outstretched fingers. Fold in half, both across and down, to find the middle, and cut a very small slit there. While it is still in half, cut sloping shoulders (Fig. 3).
8. Seam the sides to shoulder; sew shoulder seams and hem the bottom and neck. Do not finish off the neck: leave thread loose.
9. Push the head through the opening and either draw up the threads or finish off by sewing. Tie a piece of ribbon round neck to cover the join.

Collecting Coins *(for older readers)*

How to Begin

It is best to specialize in one kind of coin. You can buy a coin catalogue, which will help you decide what to go in for. You might collect a coin from every English reign since William the Conqueror, or coins from one particular century or from a foreign country, or with heraldic designs, or look for 'bun pennies' all with Queen Victoria's head on them: one for each year of her reign. 1923, 1924 and 1925 pennies are rare.

Where to Look

Jewellers' shops, antique dealers, and junk shops are good hunting grounds. You will find the value is decided not only by age but by condition and rarity.

Arranging your Collection

At first you can put each coin in an envelope, and write a short description of it on the outside. Later on you might buy a special cabinet, or find one secondhand. Cedar-wood chests are unsuitable.

Never try to clean copper coins without asking advice from an expert, but for silver coins you can use methylated spirits, ammonia or soapy water; for gold ones, lemon juice. *Never rub with anything harder than cotton wool or a soft silver brush.*

Collectors' Journals

The Royal Numismatic Society issues the *Numismatic Chronicle*, with details of classical coins, and the British Numismatic Society publishes the *British Numismatic Journal*, with information about English and Commonwealth coins.

There are good collections at the British Museum containing specimens of every kind from many countries, at the Ashmolean Museum in Oxford, the Fitzwilliam Museum in Cambridge, and the museum at Glasgow University. It is worth asking the curator at your local museum if there are any coins, as many curators keep them in special drawers.

Dance for a Party

Strip the Willow

This is an easy running-step dance for any number of couples. You can buy a record of the tune. The lines are made up into sets as follows.

	1 2 3 4 5 6 7 (girls)	
Top of dance	centre	Bottom of dance
	1 2 3 4 5 6 7 (boys)	

Holding right hands the first couple swing each other round one and a half times so that they finish with the girl facing the second boy and the boy facing the second girl.

The first girl swings the second boy round with the left hand and then comes back to the centre to swing her partner round with the right hand. She then turns the third boy with the left, then back to the centre to turn her partner with the right. (The music helps you to be in the right place at the right time.)

When the first girl reaches the bottom of the line she and her partner turn each other once more with the right hands. The boy turns the bottom girl with the left hand and his partner with the right and so on back to the top of the line.

The first couple now dance down the lines again, but *at the same time*. When they reach the bottom the set will have moved up one place. The other couples repeat the dance in turn.

Pancakes

It's much more fun if you can make these yourself, especially if you want to toss them.

You will need ¼ lb. flour, 1 egg, ½ pint milk, salt, mixing bowl, wooden spoon, palette knife, lard or butter.

1. Sift the flour into a basin with a pinch of salt. Make a well in the middle and break the egg into it.

2. Add the milk, a little at a time, stirring it into the flour. Make sure there are no lumps, then beat well – for about five minutes, until batter is creamy and bubbles appear on the surface. Stand it in a cool place for an hour or more.

3. When you are ready to start cooking, beat again for a few minutes. Melt a small knob of lard in a frying-pan and heat it until a faint smoke comes from the fat.

4. Pour in enough batter to cover the base of the pan thinly. Cook over a low heat. When set, lift carefully with a palette knife and, if it is brown, slip the knife underneath and turn it over, or try to toss it, sliding it quickly back and forth first so it does not stick.

5. When the second side of the pancake is brown turn it out on to greaseproof paper. Sprinkle with caster sugar and lemon juice, roll up, and keep warm.

Pancakes are good filled with jam or syrup, or, if you like savoury things, minced chicken, mushrooms, or grated cheese.

Outdoors

Crocuses

Spring crocuses flower this month but there is also a kind that flowers in the autumn. There are several sorts but the most common are the bright yellow and lavender ones. The funnel-shaped flowers are on long tubes that rise from narrow green leaves, like coarse grass. Watch out for jays in the garden, because they like pecking off the flowers just when they are prettiest.

This is a suitable time to spread manure over your garden and dig it well in, but do not dig near any bulbs.

Indoors

Orange, Lemon, and Grapefruit Trees

There are usually plenty of oranges, lemons, and grapefruit in the shops this month, and you may like to grow some seedlings.

Get some fine soil from the garden or, better still, buy John Innes potting compost, and fill very small flower pots with it. If you have none try plastic yogurt pots, but make a small hole in the bottom and put a few little stones in for drainage. Push three or four pips in each pot, about $\frac{1}{2}$ in. down. Keep the pots watered and in a light, warm room. When the seedlings come up, remove all but the strongest one in each pot. As these grow they may have to be replanted in a larger pot.

They won't grow any fruit, but they will look very pretty.

Making a Bird Table

Even if you have a cat, you can still have the pleasure of birds in the garden provided you give them safe nesting sites, and food and drink which is out of a cat's reach. A bird table is one of the best ways of making friends with them. Build it near a window where you can see the birds as they feed. Almost any kind of food is welcome. Provide fat, suet, cheese, bread, potatoes, and scraps and you'll find you will be serving dinner to thrushes, robins, sparrows, starlings, blackbirds, and chaffinches.

Be sure to keep a supply of water in a bowl and, when it is very cold, see that this doesn't freeze, and soak crusts in warm water. It is not a good idea to put out so much food that the birds stop searching for their own, because if you go away or forget to feed them they will suffer badly.

To encourage the tits, hang up coconuts, suet, millet sprays, and strings of nuts. Another method is to hang two plastic doilies, seamed with raffia or string and filled with lumps of fat and other scraps, from a tree. The birds will peck the food through the holes.

Materials and Tools Needed

A straight post about 5 ft long, sharpened at the lower end and with a flat top cut square across the post, a flat board about 18 in. long and 12 in. across (rectangular), one 2-in. nail, one brass cup hook, wood preservative, hammer, paint brush, heavy hammer or beetle (preferably wooden headed).

1. Drive the post into the ground with the beetle (Fig. 1).
2. Nail the board on to the top of the post by driving a nail through the centre of the board and into the centre of the top of the post (Fig. 2).
3. Screw the hook into the edge of the board near a corner to hang food from. Paint wood with preservative.

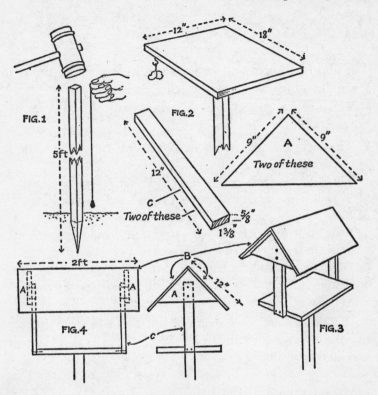

FIG.1

5ft

FIG.2

12"

18"

A

9" 9"

Two of these

C

12"

Two of these

5/8"

1 3/8"

B

12"

A

FIG.3

2ft

A A

FIG.4

C

To make a Cover to Keep the Food Dry

Materials needed: 2 plywood sheets (exterior grade) large enough (in position) to carry water clear of the table; 2 triangular gables of 1 in. plank with a right angle at the apex, 2 sides equal and shorter than the shorter side of the roof sheets; 2 pillars 12 in. × $1\frac{3}{8}$ in. × $\frac{5}{8}$ in., 2 doz. nails (1 in. ovals), tools.

1. Nail each pillar to a gable making sure the pillar is central and square and has the same overlap (Figs. 3–4).
2. Mark the position of the gable on one roof sheet. Be sure the gables will be far enough apart to allow pillars to fit just outside the table top.
3. Nail roof in position and pillars to table (Figs. 3–4).

Sevens

The idea is to throw the ball against the wall seven times, in seven different ways, and to catch it each time.

You need a rubber ball or tennis ball, a wall, flat dry ground where the ball will bounce evenly.

1. Throw it directly on to the wall and catch it without it bouncing – seven times.
2. Throw it and let it bounce once and catch it – seven times.
3. Throw it and catch it with your right hand – seven times.
4. Throw it and catch it with your left hand – seven times.
5. Raise your right leg and with your right hand throw it under your leg and up to the wall and catch it – seven times.
6. Do the same with the left leg and hand – seven times.
7. With your right hand throw the ball round your back and up to the wall and catch it – seven times.

There are lots of other ways and you can make some up yourself. But if you fail to catch a ball you have to do that particular way all over again.

March

A Spike of Green

When I went out
The sun was hot
It shone upon
My flower pot.

And there I saw
A spike of green
That no one else
Had ever seen!

On other days
The things I see
Are mostly old
Except for me.

But this green spike
So new and small
Had never yet
Been seen at all!

Barbara Baker

from All Day Long
compiled by Pamela Whitlock

Beginning of Spring

March is the month when spring begins. When hedgehogs wake from winter sleep and the fields are full of young lambs. Then the 'mad March hare' jumps about courting his mate and overhead the wild geese fly.

Easter is often in the second half of March, but its date varies according to a complicated system. Christians celebrate Christ's resurrection and give Easter eggs because eggs are a symbol of re-birth.

The Sunday before Easter is Palm Sunday. It celebrates Christ's entry into Jerusalem.

Simnel cakes are made at Easter. A man and his wife, Sim and Nell, mixed a cake and then argued about whether to boil or to bake it. Finally, they agreed to boil it first and afterwards to bake it. It turned out so well that they called it Simnel cake.

The 17 March is the feast day of St Patrick, the Patron Saint of Ireland. A legend tells how he chased all the snakes from Ireland, and it is a fact that there are no snakes there.

When March is well in it is often warm enough to play out of doors, and that is why we have suggested so many open-air things for you to do this month.

The Song Thrush

You can see and hear the song thrush all the year round.
People sometimes confuse it with the missel thrush, although
the song thrush is smaller and brighter. It has a brown back
and a buff breast with spots. It is found in gardens, woods and
hedgerows. It has a musical song which sounds rather like
'Did he do it? . . . Julie did'. It likes to eat snails. Its eggs are
turquoise blue, spotted with black. They are laid mainly in
April and May in a neatly built nest, woven from grasses,
roots, twigs and leaves, and lined with rotten wood or dung.
You will find thrushes' nests in bushes, trees and creepers.

March Flower

Wood Anemone

This is one of the earliest spring flowers, and grows, as its
name suggests, in or near woods. Its roots creep along close to
the surface of the earth, so that if you pick the flower care-
lessly the whole plant may come up in your hand. It has a
drooping bell-shaped flower with pinky-white petals, and
jagged green leaves. It is also called the windflower, because
its head turns away from any breeze.

A Guinea Pig

Guinea pigs cost anything from two shillings to several pounds. The long-haired kind are more expensive and also more difficult to rear, so it is better to choose a short-haired one. In winter it may cost from sixpence to ninepence a week to feed one, but in summer it should cost less.

Although they look so charming, guinea pigs actually belong to the rodent family. They came originally from South America. The male is known as the boar and the female as the sow. They live happily in captivity, but they have short lives, about two or three years.

Guinea pigs should be fed twice a day, with a mixture of bran, oats and fresh greens. They also like groundsel, dandelion leaves, clover, crusts, carrots, apple and potato peelings and plenty of fresh water.

Dry hay or straw makes the best bedding and should be changed every week. Cover the cage floor with sawdust. During the day put them in a moveable pen on the grass, if you can, but *be very careful not to let them overeat*. They don't like to be in the full sunlight and will catch cold if you leave them in a draught.

Guinea pigs have two or three litters a year. The babies are born, with their eyes open, after about sixty-five days. They can run about a few hours after birth and on the second day can nibble corn. They are only suckled for two weeks. It is best to separate the father when they are very young.

The most common guinea-pig sicknesses are constipation and enteritis. Constipation can be cured by extra greens, and sometimes bread and milk, but you may need to ask the advice of a veterinary surgeon about enteritis, which causes diarrhoea.

Things to Make for Easter

Easter Chickens and Ducks

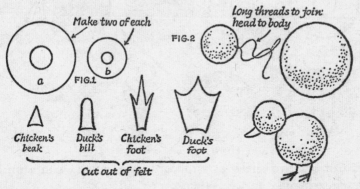

You need cardboard, yellow wool, orange felt, scissors. Make two wool balls (next page), one smaller than the other (Fig. 1). Sew together (Fig. 2). Cut out and sew on beak and feet as shown. Attach beads for eyes.

Felt Egg Cosy

You need felt scraps, scissors, needle, embroidery silk. Cut three paper patterns (Fig. 1); then cut them from felt and join them back to back with blanket stitch (Fig. 2). Blanket stitch round the bottom. Cut out three leaf shapes and sew to top (Figs. 3 and 4).

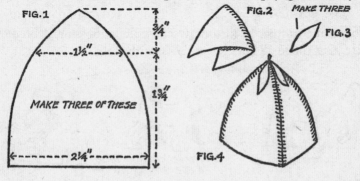

Wool Balls

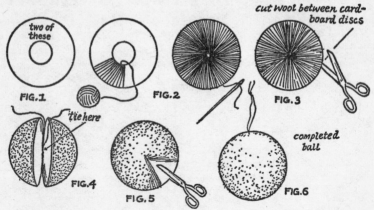

1. Cut out two circles of cardboard, 3 in. across, with a small circle inside 1 in. across (Fig. 1).
2. Wind wool round both cardboard rings until the hole in the middle becomes too small to go on. Then continue threading wool through with a darning needle (Fig. 2).
3. When the centre is too small to do this, cut the wool around the edges, between the rings (Fig. 3).
4. Tie a piece of strong thread between the rings and knot it tightly. Leave ends long enough to form a loop so you can hang the ball up.
5. Take away the cardboard and fluff out the ball.

Paper Animals

Fold some stiff paper, then draw and colour the animal on one side. Cut round all lines *except* those on the fold.

A Match-box Church

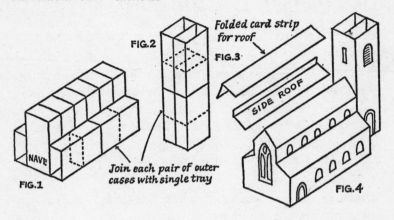

You need 14 empty match-boxes, 1 economy label, grey or white paper, scissors, glue, cardboard, paints.

1. To make the nave, place six match-boxes on top of each other, glue together and stand on end (Fig. 1).
2. Stick two more boxes on each side of the nave, removing the tray from one box and pushing the other tray half way between each box to keep firm.
3. To make the tower, glue four more boxes in two pairs, one above the other. Use the trays as before to join the pairs (Fig. 2). Stick tower to the nave.
4. To make the roof, fold in centre a piece of thin card the length of the nave and 1½ in. wide (Fig. 3).
5. Stick this to the top and keep the join in place with a piece of thin sticky paper.
6. To make the side roofs, use a piece of thin card wide enough to form the roof and overlap ¼ in. up the wall above. Glue, and cover the joins.
7. Paste white or grey paper all over the model. Paint with water colours and, when dry, make doors and windows from a different coloured paper (Fig. 4).

Decorated Easter Eggs

You will need paint-box, rag, pin, cotton, brush, needle, cup, wooden spoon.

1. Choose white eggs and wash them carefully. With a pin, make a hole at the pointed end of the egg for blowing through, and a larger one at the other end for the inside of the egg to come out.
2. Gently blow the egg out of the shell into a cup. Keep the inside for making scrambled eggs (see below).
3. Decorate the egg-shells with patterns, faces, names, etc.

Coloured Eggs

Boil the eggs in water containing a little vinegar and some cooking colouring: a teaspoon to ¾ pint of water.

Initialled Eggs

1. Melt a little cooking-fat or candle grease and use it to draw on the name or initials you want to appear.
2. Leave to harden and then soak the egg in vinegar for about half an hour.
3. Boil the egg in water and colouring, and the name written on it will appear against the colour.

An Easter Tree

Find a nicely shaped branch or twig, about three feet high; plant it in a pot and hang your eggs and chickens on it.

Scrambled Eggs for Breakfast

You need eggs, salt, pepper, milk, margarine or butter.

1. Break one egg for each person into a bowl. Add a tablespoon of milk for each egg and beat well with a whisk or fork. Add salt and pepper to taste.
2. Melt a knob of margarine or butter over a low heat in a thick saucepan and pour in the eggs. Stir gently until it is thick and creamy. Spoon out of the saucepan *at once*, or it will go on cooking.

March Out of Doors

A Nature Diary

It is interesting to keep a Nature Diary. You can use an exercise book, or, if you like drawing, make your own album with alternate pages of plain and lined paper (see p. 128 for instructions).

It is best to start each month on a new page, and design a suitable heading, or else press the month's flower and mount it at the beginning. Remember to date and label each entry, and if you are really enthusiastic, leave enough room for each month to make a five-year diary. Then you can compare your entries from year to year. For example, in April one year the ground may be covered with several inches of snow, while another year the daffodils will be flowering.

Check the truth of some of these old weather sayings:

A red sky at night is a shepherd's delight,
A red sky in the morning is a shepherd's warning.

If the oak is out before the ash
Then you may expect a splash;
If the ash is out before the oak
Then you may expect a soak.

If the rooks build high the weather will be dry.

Rain before seven, fine before eleven.

If the north wind blows on Michaelmas Day (29 *September*)
The month of October is sunny and gay.

St Swithin's Day if thou dost rain (15 *July*)
For forty days it will remain.

So many fogs in March, so many frosts in May.

Ice in November will bear a duck,
February weather all mire and muck.

March Buds

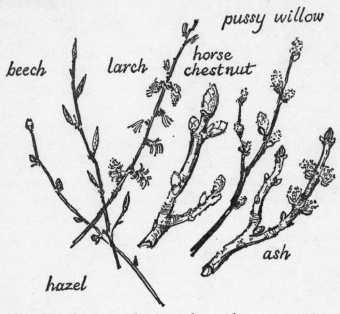

This is a lovely time of year to learn about trees. Here are some of the buds you can look for.

Pussy Willow
A small tree which has its flowers before the leaves. The young twigs and buds are covered with small hairs, the buds are small and brown until the large male catkins (with long, silky hairs of a cheerful yellow colour) and the small, thin, grey female catkins, burst out of them.

Hazel
A large shrub, often found in oak woods or hedges. Has smooth brown stems, with hairy twigs, leaves and stalks. The male catkins (or lambs' tails) are long and yellow, with pollen before the leaves are out, while the female flowers are enclosed by small brown bracts with a tuft of red at the top.

Horse Chestnut

Is easily recognized by its large, smooth sticky buds and the horse-shoe shaped scars on its twigs, showing where leaves have fallen off. If you pick the twigs before the buds have opened, and put them in water, you will see the leaves gradually unfurl.

Ash

A tall tree, with grey, grooved trunk, this has smooth grey twigs and distinctive jet black buds, very tightly closed and small, growing in pairs opposite each other on the branches.

Beech

Has a straight trunk and smooth grey bark, with very long, pointed soft brown buds, shaped like cigars.

Larch

This is the only British conifer which loses all its leaves in the autumn. It looks bare in winter, but is very pretty in the spring, when it grows sharp pointed tufts of leaves on very short shoots; female cones are pink, and male cones yellow.

Squirrels

There are both red and grey squirrels in the British Isles, but the native red squirrels are growing scarce. In many districts, especially in southern England, the American grey squirrel is replacing them.

Squirrels are very timid and when they are frightened they chatter and scold. They are very agile and leap about the trees and race head-first down the trunks. They are also very industrious and thrifty and collect hundreds of nuts which they store for the winter in holes in the ground. Unfortunately they have bad memories and often forget the place.

By February or March both kinds of squirrel are busy building nests. Red squirrels prefer conifers or hollows in other trees, and build more nests close to the first to move the young into if there is any danger. Grey squirrels prefer deciduous trees. Squirrels' nests have a domed roof and a side entrance.

Red squirrels often have two litters, in March or April and in August, but grey squirrels may have three. Baby squirrels are born naked and blind.

March Hares

The hare does not live in a burrow like a rabbit but lies crouched in the open in a 'form' most of the day and night. It moves by making a series of jumps with its hind legs and skips with its forelegs; the faster it goes the longer are its jumps.

Male hares are called 'Jacks'. They court the 'does', female hares, in February and March. Then they become very excited and run about kicking, bucking and jumping, and this is why people say 'mad as March hares'.

The doe has litters twice a year. She usually has between two and five babies, called 'leverets'. She is a very good mother and will fight bravely to protect her young. Soon after the leverets are born the doe finds separate forms for each one and at night visits each in turn to suckle it. After about a month the leverets are strong enough to fend for themselves.

Badgers

Badgers do their spring cleaning in March. They live in burrows, called 'sets', made in banks or rocky hills. The set has one or more rooms and several entrance passages. At the main entrance there is always a large mound of soil which the badger has dug out when making it. They are very clean and always wipe their paws on a tree before entering their home.

When they do their spring cleaning they pull their bedding

out into the sun, dig a new chamber, and line it with fresh grass and ferns ready for the family they will have in spring or summer. The cubs are silver grey. They are born blind and helpless and are looked after by their mother, who washes and feeds them until they are two months old and strong enough to leave home.

Badgers sleep during the day and for most of the winter. At night they come out to look for food and to play. They eat practically anything: insects, snakes, young birds, rabbits, moles, as well as roots, fruit, honey, slugs and snails.

Freshwater Shells

Shells can be found in rivers, streams, ponds, lakes and ditches, as well as in the sea, and the best time to search for them is on a warm sunny day when there is only a slight breeze. If the water is clear you will be able to see the shells lying on the bottom, but if it is muddy you will need to dredge for them. If you have no net an ordinary household sieve or colander will do. Take a collecting tin or jar to bring the shells home. Put some leaves on the bottom to avoid breaking them. The following are a few of the commonest freshwater shells you may find:

Water Snails

1. The great pond snail, which is found in large ponds and slowly flowing rivers.
2. The dwarf pond snail, found at the edge of small ditches and swampy pastures.
3. The wandering snail, which is very common and found almost everywhere.
4. The valve snail, in streams and slow-running rivers.
5. The common river snail, one of the largest.
6. The marsh lymnaea, on the mud beside pools and ditches.

C

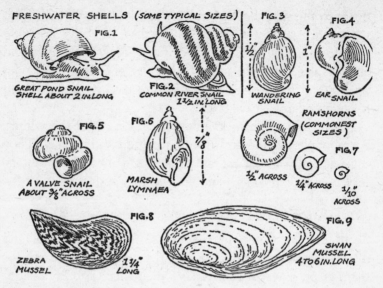

FRESHWATER SHELLS (SOME TYPICAL SIZES)

FIG.1 GREAT POND SNAIL SHELL ABOUT 2 IN. LONG

FIG.2 COMMON RIVER SNAIL 1½ IN. LONG

FIG.3 WANDERING SNAIL 1½"

FIG.4 EAR SNAIL 1"

FIG.5 A VALVE SNAIL ABOUT ⅜" ACROSS

FIG.6 MARSH LYMNAEA ⅞"

RAMSHORNS (COMMONEST SIZES) ½" ACROSS

FIG.7 ¼" ACROSS 1/10" ACROSS

FIG.8 ZEBRA MUSSEL 1¼" LONG

FIG.9 SWAN MUSSEL 4 TO 6 IN. LONG

Flat Coil Snails

There are several kinds of ramshorn snail, which are found in widely distributed ponds, and ditches, sometimes floating on the surface.

Freshwater Mussels

1. The zebra mussel is like the common mussel but has a distinctive pattern on its shell and is often found clinging to submerged objects in rivers, canals and locks.
2. The swan mussel, found in slow water and ponds, usually in large numbers.

Try to find empty shells, but if you do find one with a living creature inside, remove it before you add the shell to your collection. Wash the shells in warm water and dry them gently. Paint them thinly with white of egg to keep them shiny. Label your collection and keep on cotton wool in small cardboard boxes.

Brass Rubbing

If you look at the stone floors in old churches you will often see brass pictures set into them. From these you can learn interesting things about people who lived between the thirteenth and eighteenth centuries.

To take brass rubbings you will need a roll of white paper – such as ceiling paper – a stick of heelball from a cobbler, a duster, a soft nail-brush, and weights – such as hassocks.

1. You must first ask permission from the Rector or Vicar. There may be a small fee to pay, particularly if it is a very special brass. Choose a small brass for your first attempt, and dust it.
2. Unroll the paper over the brass and weight down the corners firmly with hassocks or books, but NOT hymn books.
3. Rub over the paper gently with the soft nail-brush to show the outline.
4. Using the flat of the heelball (not the sharp edge) rub steadily and evenly all over the brass.
5. Label and date the rubbing.
6. Roll up the paper and put away anything you have moved.

Bark Rubbing

You will need a carpenter's pencil, white paper (not too thick), 4 drawing-pins or some sticky tape.

1. Choose a tree with a smooth bark.
2. Attach your paper with drawing-pins or tape at each corner.
3. Rub across the paper in smooth lines with the side of your pencil, not pressing too hard.
4. Carefully remove the paper from the tree. Label, then mount in your scrapbook or nature diary, leaving space to add stencils of dried leaves and drawings of seeds from the same tree.

March Gardening

Outdoors

This month is known for its blustering winds. These help to dry the soil, so that you may now be able to sow a few lettuce or radish seeds. You can buy some packets of early varieties very cheaply, and follow the instructions they give.

Herb Tubs

You can make a herb garden in an old zinc bath or sink. Stand the container on bricks to raise it. Cover the bottom with a layer of stones to let the water drain through, and then fill it with ordinary garden soil, sieved if possible. Some leaf mould from a wood helps to enrich the soil and stops it from becoming dry and hard.

Buy packets of parsley, thyme and borage seed from a gardening shop and perhaps you could ask a friend for a small plant or cuttings of sage and chives. There is an old belief that if you are feeling unhappy the borage plant will help make you glad again, and its pretty purple leaves look very gay.

Indoors

Cactus Plants

Cactus plants start to grow again in March. Loosen the soil on the surface of the pots to let the air reach the roots. Put the plants in a light, sunny place.

You can buy a special kind of soil for cacti quite cheaply. It is a good idea to re-pot your plants in this once a year, changing all the soil except that clinging to the roots. Some of the plants may need larger pots.

Games to Play

Pig in the Middle

You need three players and a ball.

The players stand in a row, as far apart as they wish, with one at each end, and one in the middle.

The outside players have to throw the ball to each other while the 'Pig', or middle player, tries to catch the ball himself. As soon as he does, he changes places with the player who threw the ball, who then becomes 'Pig' in the middle.

Beetle

You need one dice, paper and a pencil for each player (any number of players).

Each player throws the dice and the first to throw a six starts the game. Then each player in turn throws the dice, and draws the part of a beetle which his dice number allows. Go on throwing in turn until one player has drawn a whole beetle. He is the winner.

Rules:

6 – to start the game	3 – feet and hands
6 – body	2 – eyes
5 – head	1 – nose and mouth
4 – arms and legs	

Animal Snap

You need a pack of playing cards, any number of players.

This game is for players of any age. If there are more than five or six players, you need two packs of playing cards.

Each player decides which animal he will be, cat, dog, cow,

duck, hen or pig, etc. The cards are dealt round to each player, who keeps them face downwards in front of him. The player on the left of the dealer turns over the top card from his pile, placing it face upwards on the table in front of him. The other players in the same way. When a card is turned up that 'matches' any of the other cards on the table, the two players concerned have to make the noise of each other's animals. For example – if the player representing the 'cow' turns up a card which matches the card in front of the player representing the 'duck', the cow player must 'quack' and the duck player must 'moo'. The player who makes the correct noise first gives his face-up pile to the other player. The winner is the player who loses his cards first.

Matchstick Tower

You need a pile of match sticks and an egg-cup. See how many matches you can place on top of the cup before they fall off. Lay the matches in a diamond or square to start and build up from these.

This can also be played as a team game. After a given period the team with the biggest pile wins.

'O'Grady Says'

(four or more can play this game)

One player is chosen as 'O'Grady' and the others have to do what he says. For example, 'O'Grady says touch your head', 'O'Grady says sit down', 'O'Grady says hands up'.

Everyone does as bidden unless the words 'O'Grady says' are omitted.

If played with a small group, the one to make a mistake becomes 'O'Grady', but if played with a large number of children, those who go wrong are out, the last one being the winner.

Skipping

Once you have learned to do ordinary skipping try something more complicated. There are many old skipping rhymes. Here are some for several children skipping together. In each of them, two turn the rope, while the others run in and skip in turn.

In the first, while one player skips over the rope, the rest all chant: 'Salt, mustard, vinegar, pepper'. When it has been repeated three times, she runs out and the next player runs in to take her place.

Teddy Bear, Teddy Bear

This is an action rhyme, the player performing the actions as she skips, while the other players join in the chant.

Teddy bear, teddy bear, touch the ground (*touch the ground with hand*)

Teddy bear, teddy bear, turn right round (*turn right round*)

Teddy bear, teddy bear, go upstairs (*legs moved up and down as though mounting stairs*)

Teddy bear, teddy bear, say your prayers (*hands held as in prayer*)

Teddy bear, teddy bear, turn off the light (*hand switches off light*)

Teddy bear, teddy bear, say 'Good Night' (*hands together at side of the head*)

March Games

Doctor, Doctor

The rope-turners say the first and third lines, and the skipper the second and fourth lines, running out when the rhyme is over.

Doctor, doctor, how's your wife?
Very bad, upon my life.
Can she eat a bit of pie?
Yes she can, as well as I.

Birthdays

The players call out the months of the year, January, February, March and so on. Each player skips until her birthday month is called, when she must run out and another player takes her place.

If the rope is long enough, this can be played by several players skipping at the same time.

Counting Rhymes

As the player skips, the turners say:

Baby in the cradle, fast asleep
How many hours does she sleep?

or

One o'clock, two o'clock, three o'clock, four,
Five o'clock, six o'clock, seven o'clock, more.

The rope is then turned as quickly as possible, and the number of hours are the number of skips the player can finish before she is out.

In the last three, the players turning the rope call out:

'U.N.D.E.R. spells under', and on the word under, the player must run under the rope and out the other side, or

'O.V.E.R. spells over', when the player must run and jump over the rope and out again, or

'I.N. spells in', when the player must run in and start skipping to one of the rhymes given above or any other one they may choose.

April

The Thrush's Nest

Within a thick and spreading hawthorn bush
That overhung a mole-hill large and round,
I heard from morn to morn a merry thrush
Sing hymns to sunrise, and I drank the sound
With joy; and, often an intruding guest,
I watched her secret toils from day to day –
How true she warped the moss to form a nest,
And modelled it within the wood and clay;
And by and by, like heath-bells gilt with dew,
There lay her shining eggs, as bright as flowers,
Ink-spotted over shells of greeny blue;
And there I witnessed, in the sunny hours,
A brood of nature's minstrels chirp and fly,
Glad as that sunshine and the laughing sky.

John Clare

The Cuckoo's Month

Everyone knows that 1 April is All Fools' Day – when people try to trick each other. It has been suggested that the reason for this strange custom is that it was the day when Noah sent the dove from the Ark and it came back without being able to find land. So now the best April fool jokes are to do with 'sending on a fool's errand'. After noon, the joke rebounds on the joker, and the intended victim can retort 'April Fools' Day's past and gone, You're the fool and I'm none'.

The song of the cuckoo is first heard in April and there is an ancient saying that if a girl wants to know how many years it will be before she marries, she can count the answer in the number of 'cuckoo' calls she hears. For boys the cuckoo's call means that all the adventures of summer are beginning.

April is famous for its showers, so we have made an extra long list of things to make indoors in case you can't go out very often.

Blackbird

The blackbird is a very common bird and can be seen throughout the year. But its sweet song seems most joyous in April. It also has a harsh alarm note 'chuk, chuk'.

The male is glossy black with a yellow bill, but the female is browner with a brown bill. Sometimes blackbirds have patches of white, more rarely they are completely white. After landing on the ground the blackbird's tail is often raised and he will hop, not run, across the ground. His nest, like that of the song thrush, is usually made in a bush, creeper, or tree. The eggs are pale blue mottled with brown.

April Flower

Primrose

Long ago all flowers were called roses, and the primrose comes so early in the year that it was called 'first rose', or primrose. The flowers are a pale yellow, and grow on a pink hairy stalk among wrinkled leaves. They grow in woods and hedgerows, fields and gardens. They have a faint sweet fresh smell which is the very essence of spring.

Where there are plenty you may take up some roots for your garden, or to be potted with earth and moss.

A Muscovy Duck

This month's pet is rather an unusual one, and is only possible if you live in the country and have plenty of room.

Muscovy ducks are very handsome black-and-white birds with red beaks. They soon let you know whether they are pleased or annoyed, by the way they make the crest of feathers on their head stand up or lie down.

They like water, but a very little is ample, and a pair of ducks will be content with a baby bath. They usually prefer to make their nest under a hedge or a bush in the garden, but it is sometimes a good idea to provide a small wooden house for them.

They need feeding twice a day, a handful of corn at one meal and some wet poultry meal with potato peelings mixed into it at the next.

They breed twice a year, and the hen sits on the eggs for six weeks before the ducklings hatch. These are enchanting to watch as they waddle anxiously after their parents. You may find it advisable to clip the parents' wings in the spring, as they tend to stray and might disappear into neighbouring gardens.

Things to Make and Do

Things to Make with Boxes and Tins

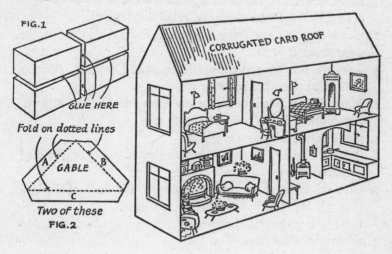

FIG. 1

GLUE HERE

Fold on dotted lines

A GABLE B

C

Two of these
FIG. 2

CORRUGATED CARD ROOF

A Shoe-Box House

You need four shoe-boxes, ruler and pencil, plain and corrugated cardboard, glue and brush, scissors.

1. Make sure the boxes are all the same size. Then glue each pair end to end.
2. Put one pair on top of the other and glue in position (Fig. 1).
3. Cut 2 large triangles of cardboard and shape to make the gables (Fig. 2). The pieces marked A, B and C are folded inwards. C is stuck to the top shoe box, A and B are to support the roof.
4. Cut a piece of corrugated cardboard the same length as the boxes, and twice the length of side A in width.
5. Cut out windows, or else paint them on.

A Market Stall

You need one square sugar-cube box, four or five match-box trays, pencil, rubber, glue, paints, plasticine.

1. Rule a line ½ in. up from the bottom along one side of the box. Mark one end A, the other B, then cut down the two sides to A and B. Bend over along the ruled line (Fig. 1).
2. Cut a diagonal line from A to point C (Fig. 1), then do the same from B to D.
3. Take the box lid and cut up the short end marked 'perforation'. Cut the other end to match.
4. Measure ¾ in. from the top on one long side. Cut the strip off, cut this strip in half, and keep both safe.
5. Cut a fringe as shown in Fig. 2.
6. Paint all the pieces, or cover them with wall-paper or gummed coloured paper.
7. Glue the back of the canopy firmly to the back of the box (Fig. 3). When dry, bend the canopy over.
8. Put a little glue on the bottom of both long strips and fasten to the inside of the front (Fig. 4).
9. Now bend the canopy so that the front edge touches the top of the supports and glue to the inside.
10. Fix match-box trays along the stall with plasticine. Make your 'goods' – meat, fish, or cakes – with coloured dough or plasticine. Make flowers with coloured paper.

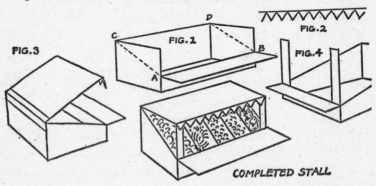

FIG.3   FIG.1   FIG.2   FIG.4

COMPLETED STALL

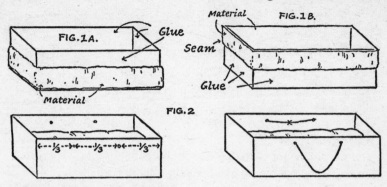

A Carry Cot For Your Doll

You need a shoe box, length of material, scissors, needle and cotton, string, glue, paper and pencil.

1. Measure a piece of material large enough to go round the box, with 1 in. over for turnings. Join the two ends.

2. Fold the loop of material in half lengthways, and ease on to the box with the inside facing out (see Fig. 1A).

3. Put some glue on the top half of the outside of the box. Turn up the folded half of the material and press it down on to the part you have glued.

4. Fold up the other half of the material (Fig. 1B). Glue the bottom half of the box and fold the material down on to the glue as in the top half.

5. Mark inside the box with a pencil and make a small hole $\frac{1}{2}$ in. below the top of the box and a third of the length of the box from each end (Fig. 2).

6. Cut two lengths of cord, string or ribbon to make a convenient handle and thread through the holes each side.

7. To make sheets and blankets for the cot, use old scraps of big ones. Measure the length and width of the cot, and add half as much again.

8. To make a mattress or pillow, measure two pieces of sheet the length and width of your cot and add 1 in. all round for turnings. Turn inside out and sew on three sides. Turn, and stuff. Turn in the edges of the remaining side and oversew.

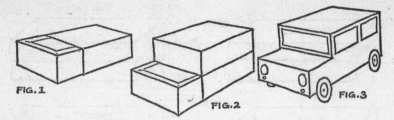

FIG. 1 FIG. 2 FIG. 3

A Match-Box Car

You need one empty match-box and the inner tray of one other, scissors, glue, coloured paper, small piece of cardboard.

1. Slide the tray of the match-box forward so that it is about half way out of the cover and turn it upside down (Fig. 1).
2. Stick it in this position with a length of dark blue or black paper.
3. Stick the other tray upside down on top to form the roof of the car (Fig. 2). Paste pieces of coloured paper over the joins and over the open end of the box.
4. Paint on windows or stick on squares of white paper, and stick on a thick strip of paper to form the roof.
5. To make the wheels, draw round a sixpence on stiff cardboard and cut them out. Paste these circles to the box (Fig. 3).

A Match-Box Lorry

You need one match-box cover, three match-box trays, cork (for wheels), six brass paper-fasteners, scissors, knife, pins, fine steel knitting-needle.

1. Cut four rings from the cork about ⅛ in. thick for the wheels.
2. Bore holes through rings with knitting-needle.
3. Fix two wheels into the back of the match-box cover with brass paper-fasteners (Fig. 1).
4. Fix the other two cork wheels into the front of one of the match-box trays in the same way (Fig. 2).
5. Slide this tray about half-way into the cover and you have the 'chassis'.
6. Make the 'cab' of the lorry from a second tray. Cut out about ½ in. from the base of the tray, leaving the two side pieces. Cut

out another small piece from the rest of the base for the wind-screen (Fig. 3).

7. This tray will now sit firmly on the 'chassis', the two side pieces gripping the front part of the match-box cover.

8. Now slip the final tray on to the back part of the 'chassis' and fix to the 'cab' by paper-fasteners (Fig. 4).

Pin on extras such as a steering wheel, spare tyres, or number plate made from more pieces of cork or card.

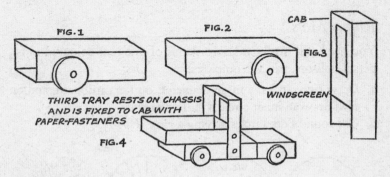

A Rattling Roller

This is a good toy for a baby sister or brother who has just learned to walk.

1. Make a hole in each end of a tin.

2. Put five or six pebbles inside and replace the lid.

3. Bend a piece of wire, about 16 in. long, into a loop in the centre. Make a right angle 2 in. from each end and then bend again.

4. Push the ends of the wire through the holes in the tin.

5. Tie a piece of string to the loop. The toy will make a clanking noise as it is pulled along.

A Toy Telephone For a Young Brother or Sister

This is a simple telephone to make from two empty chocolate or coffee tins and a long piece of string.

April Indoors

1. Make a hole in the end of each tin by hammering a nail through it.
2. Thread the string through the hole and tie a large knot at the end of it, so that it stays inside the tin.
3. Stretch the string so that it is quite taut and you will find that by speaking quietly into the tin at one end you will be heard quite clearly at the other. The important thing is to have long narrow tins and to keep the string very tight.

Raffia Mats

You need stiff cardboard, two skeins of different coloured raffia, pencil, scissors, pair of compasses.

1. Draw two circles, 7 in. in diameter, on the cardboard, and on each draw an inner circle 2 in. in diameter.
2. Cut round both circles leaving a ring (Fig. 1).

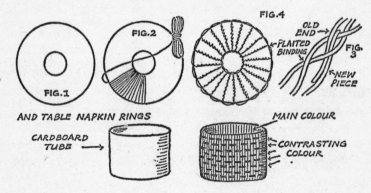

FIG.4

OLD END →

← PLAITED BINDING

FIG. 3

← NEW PIECE

FIG.2

FIG.1

AND TABLE NAPKIN RINGS

CARDBOARD TUBE →

MAIN COLOUR

← CONTRASTING COLOUR

3. Put these two rings together and, taking a skein of raffia, wind it round the rings of cardboard (Fig. 2). Overlap the strands of raffia so that they cover the cardboard very thickly. To join the raffia, knot the ends together and cover the knot with the new strand. Continue until the whole ring is covered. Finish off with a needle, threading the end of the raffia underneath another strand.
4. Take three strands of a different coloured raffia and plait them

together, making a plait 3 yds long. You will have to join fresh strands of raffia into the plait as it grows. Be careful never to join in three strands at the same place or your plait will become lumpy. Join by laying a new piece alongside the end of the old one and working the two together for two stitches. Cut off the old end and continue with the new (Fig. 3).

When the plait is finished, pin one end of it to the edge of the inner circle and sew around the mat with a blanket stitch. When you come to the beginning sew the two ends together and cut off any remaining ends of raffia which may be showing (Fig. 4).

Raffia Skirt

Here are two ways of making raffia skirts.

To Make a Quick Skirt

Take a length of tape two feet longer than your waist measurement, fold the raffia in half over the tape and tie it round you.

To Make a More Lasting Skirt

You need a tape 1 in. wide and the length of your waist plus 8 in. at each end. Fold the strands of raffia in half and stick them over the tape by putting a little glue on one surface and pressing the raffia down on to it with a clean rag. You can either stick another piece of tape over the top or thread a needle with raffia and stitch along the top of the band through the raffia and tape.

And of course you do the same thing to make a skirt for a doll.

A Doll's Dinner (Not Edible)

You need 3 cupfuls flour, 3 teaspoonsful salt, 3 or 4 drops of cochineal or one teaspoonful poster paint, water, basin.

1. Put the flour, salt, and colouring in the basin and mix with a little water until it forms a ball which does not stick to the basin or to your hands. If you have made it too wet add more flour.
2. Now you can model it into cakes, fruit, hams, pies, or

77

whatever you like. If you make everything small enough it will be the right size for your dolls' house or shop.

3. Bake in a moderate oven, regulo 4, 355° F, until they are hard. When cold, paint them the right colours.

Newspaper Clothes

Dressing up in newspaper is a good way to spend a wet afternoon. All you need is: large newspapers, pins, a friend. No scissors are allowed, and all fitting is done by tearing and pinning.

For a Skirt. Use a large sheet of newspaper. Fold along the top to give the right length and then pin the two edges together. Ask your friend to hold it firmly at her waist while you pin in pleats so that it fits without sliding off. You can put in one large pleat at the back and front, or small ones all round. You can make it look ragged by tearing chunks out at the hem and slitting upwards.

A Tunic Top is made by folding a large double sheet of paper in half. Tear out a semi-circle at the centre of the fold. Slip this over your friend's head, pin up the sides under the arms (point downwards always) and gather in at the waist with a rolled 'belt' of paper. Cross bands can be made by folding the paper into wide strips and tucking the lower end into the belt or skirt while the top is pinned to the shoulders.

Making newspaper clothes is a good game to play at a party. Work in pairs and see which pair produces the best outfit in five minutes.

Covering Books

You need thin cartridge paper, polythene, adhesive tape, scissors, glue, ruler.

1. If the book has a paper jacket, remove and measure it. If not, measure the book itself and add 2 in. each end.

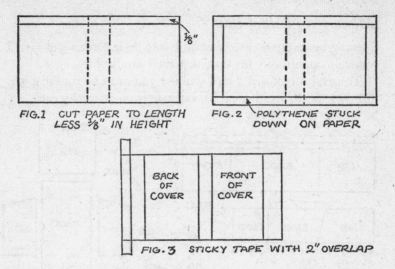

FIG. 1 CUT PAPER TO LENGTH LESS ⅜" IN HEIGHT

FIG. 2 POLYTHENE STUCK DOWN ON PAPER

BACK OF COVER

FRONT OF COVER

FIG. 3 STICKY TAPE WITH 2" OVERLAP

2. Cut a piece of paper the same size, less ⅛ in. in height (Fig. 1).
3. Cut a piece of polythene 1 in. wider and ½ in. longer than the paper.
4. Lay the paper on the polythene and stick the long edges of the polythene over the top with glue or adhesive tape (Fig. 2).
5. When this is dry, slip the paper jacket from the book into the tube formed by the paper and polythene. If you fold it loosely in half and slide it in the centre, you will find it goes in quite easily.
6. Lay the cover down, polythene side uppermost, and stick a length of adhesive tape along the edge of the back flap (Fig. 3). Overlap 2 in. each end.
7. Put the cover on the book and stick the ends of the tape to the hard cover of the book. The front flap can be stuck in the same way or just folded under.

If you have books which have lost their paper covers you could make new covers for them using coloured or patterned paper under the polythene.

Making a Nesting Box

Nesting boxes attract breeding birds into your garden and give a valuable opportunity for watching their family life.

To make a box that a bird will use you must be sure that it is firmly secured, weather-proof, and safe from attack by cats.

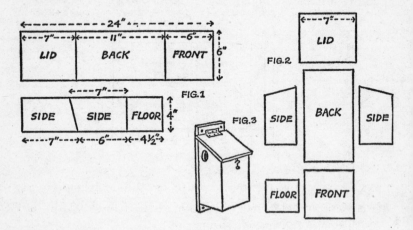

The following details are for a top-opening box to be made in three stages from two pieces of wood 24 in. by 6 in. by ¾ in., and 17½ in. by 4 in. by ¾ in. These are marked and cut up as shown in Figs. 1 and 2 and then assembled with nails or screws; 1¼-in. brass or galvanized fixings will be best as the box must withstand the weather. A hook and screw eye are needed for the lid, and a hinge. The entrance hole is illustrated on one of the side panels (Fig. 3). If it is made in the front panel below the insertion for the screw eye, it may be rather low down for species which build substantial nests. Some observers, however, prefer to put it in front to gain shelter from the overhanging roof and make the hole (1¼ in. diameter) in one of the top corners to avoid the screw eye.

The British Trust for Ornithology (Tring) publish a booklet giving details of boxes of all kinds.

Coconut Ice
Peppermint Creams

Coconut Ice

You need 1 lb. granulated sugar, ½ lb. of desiccated coconut, thick saucepan, greaseproof paper, ¼ pint of milk, cochineal or other colouring, baking tin.

1. Butter, and then line a baking tin with greaseproof paper.
2. Put the sugar and milk in a thick saucepan. Boil them for about 3 minutes.
3. Remove saucepan from stove, add coconut, stirring all the time. Then put in cochineal, a drop at a time, until it is the shade of pink you like.
4. Pour the mixture into the tin and leave in a cool place to set.
5. When set, cut into bars, and if there's any left at the end of the day, store it in an airtight tin.

Peppermint Creams

You need ½ lb. icing sugar, 1 teaspoonful of peppermint essence, pastry cutter, 1 egg white, large bowl, pastry board.

1. Sift the sugar into the basin.
2. Beat the egg white until stiff and add the sugar. Add the peppermint essence and mix well until a stiff paste is formed.
3. Sprinkle a board with icing sugar and roll out the paste until it is about ¼ in. thick.
4. Cut out into rounds with a small pastry cutter and leave on a wire tray for twelve to twenty-four hours till firm.

Games to Play

Patience

One pack of playing cards, one player.

This is just the thing to play when you are alone, or in bed. Put out nine cards, face upwards, in three rows of three cards each. The aim is to pair off the cards so that you finish with no cards in your hands. Each pair must total eleven. The court cards count as eleven each and an ace counts as one.

You can take your first pair which add up to eleven (or a royal card) from the cards face upwards on the table and put them down. Then fill the two spaces from the pack in your hand (which is face downwards) so that you again have nine cards on the table – and so on until the pack is finished.

If you have nine cards on the table and cannot see a pair which add up to eleven and have not a royal card which you can discard, you must start all over again!

Letter Words

You need paper, pencils, any number of players.

The first person calls the name of a country, for example Australia. Everyone else writes down the name of another country which begins with the last letter of the previous country called, in this case 'A'. Then the person on the left of the first caller calls out another country, and everyone writes down, as before, a country starting with the final letter of the country called. The game continues till each person has called a country.

You can also play this game with the names of towns, rivers, animals, or plants.

Marbles

The Roman Emperor Augustus played marbles, so it is an ancient game. Ordinary marbles are called *commoneys*, *potteys* or *stoneys*, and it is these which are shot at *alleys* (the best kind, formerly made of alabaster), or at the precious *blood alley*, a large marble streaked with red. Usually a *stoney* is worth three *commoneys* or two *potteys*, an *alley* is worth four *potteys* or six *commoneys*, and a *blood alley* in good condition can be exchanged for anything between twelve to fifty *commoneys*.

Boss-Out (two players)
One player rolls a marble and, when it stops, the second player tries to hit it with one of his. If he succeeds, he takes the original marble; if not, the first player rolls a marble at his opponent's. When a marble is lost, the owner must retire, or produce another.

Knock-Out (old marbles, two to five players)
Each player in turn throws a marble against a wall. When one marble hits another, the thrower picks up all the marbles on the ground. This is fun, but use old marbles, as they chip easily.

There are other marble games you can find out about.

The Farmer's in His Den

This can be played indoors and outdoors, by boys and girls. The children make a circle round one child, 'the Farmer', who stands in the middle. The circle join hands and walk round the Farmer singing:

> The Farmer's in his den
> The Farmer's in his den
> Heigh-ho, heigh-ho
> The Farmer's in his den.
>
> The Farmer wants a wife
> The Farmer wants a wife
> Heigh-ho, heigh-ho
> The Farmer wants a wife.

The circle stops and the Farmer chooses one child from the circle to be his 'wife' and she joins him in the centre, the circle join hands again and walk round the Farmer and his Wife, singing:

> The Wife wants a child
> The Wife wants a child
> Heigh-ho, heigh-ho,
> The Wife wants a child.

The Wife now chooses someone from the circle to be her child. The game goes on in the same way with everyone singing this verse:

> The Child wants a nurse
> The Child wants a nurse
> Heigh-ho, heigh-ho
> The Child wants a nurse.

Then they sing:

> The Nurse wants a dog
> The Nurse wants a dog
> Heigh-ho, heigh-ho
> The Nurse wants a dog.

Then finally:

> We all pat the Dog
> We all pat the Dog
> Heigh-ho, heigh-ho
> We all pat the Dog.

Everyone then pats the Dog, who is the Farmer next time if you play the game again.

Card Building

You need a pack of playing cards, patience, and a firm surface (preferably non-slip) on which to build. You can also build on a carpeted floor, away from draughts.

Start with a basic formation which can be enlarged upwards and outwards. Balance cards as shown in Figs. 1, 2, and 3. You can make several of these buildings close together and join them by laying cards along the side. Build another layer on top in the

 same way and another on top of that.

FIG.1   FIG.2   FIG.3

Using a Library

There is a children's section in most libraries, where the books will be divided into groups such as fiction, hobbies, travel, natural history, history, music, and so on. Once you have joined the library you may borrow books from these shelves, and take them home for two or three weeks. Always remember to look after the books very carefully.

There are also shelves of reference books, encyclopedias and dictionaries, for you to read in the library, but not to take away.

The librarians are there to advise you and to help you find your books, and they will order books you want to borrow if they are not already in the library.

April

Indoor and Outdoor Gardening

A Water Garden

You need a jar; water-glass; crystals of alum, iron sulphate, copper sulphate; water; silver sand. You can order the crystals from a chemist and the sand from a shop selling fish as pets. Fill any jar or bottle about three quarters full of warm water, then add the water-glass, stirring and shaking until the solution is cold. Put fine silver sand in the jar and let it sink to the bottom, forming a layer an inch thick. Then press a few of each of the crystals into the sand, so that they are out of sight (use a knitting needle). Take care not to spill or jog the water, and in a few days the crystals will rise in the liquid in strings of lovely colour.

Writing with Flowers

To write your name in flowers, choose a small flower like Virginia stock. Rake and smooth the soil well and manure it. Mark out your name with a stick in letters 6 in. high.

You may need more than one packet of seeds. Empty the seeds on to a saucer so that you can divide them up equally for each letter. Then sow them according to the instructions on the packet.

This month sow sweet peas. With their gay colours and sweet scent they are lovely for cutting later. Sow them in flower pots and keep indoors. Plant them out in early June, with some twiggy sticks to climb up.

It is also the time to plant marrow seeds, following the instructions on the packet.

May

And after April, when May follows,
And the white throat builds, and all
the swallows!
Hark, where my blossom'd pear tree
in the hedge
Leans to the field and scatters on the
clover
Blossoms and dewdrops –

Robert Browning

Going
A-Maying

May is the merry month when there have always been cele-
brations to welcome the summer.

In the reign of Elizabeth I on May Day the village chose
the prettiest girl for May Queen. Then the boys and girls
went a-maying. They gathered flowers and, to the jolly
music of the horn and tabor, paraded through the streets,
calling at each house to decorate it.

On the village green there was the maypole with multi-
coloured ribbons hanging from it, and the children danced
round holding these, and plaiting them into patterns as they
went, and sometimes there was a hobby horse, a brightly
decorated canvas horse about six feet long which was paraded
through the town, to the roll of drums.

Maypoles are still put up on some village greens and each
year there is a parade at Minehead in Somerset and also at
Padstow, where the hobby horse wears a fantastic mask and is
called an 'obby oss'. In London on May Day there is a parade
of decorated horses in Hyde Park.

The Swallow

The swallow is one of our best known summer visitors and is seen most frequently between May and September. Its slender build, long wings and forked tail make it easily recognizable. It has a blue-black sheen on the upper parts, long tail feathers, white-to-buff underparts, a chestnut forehead and throat with a dark blue band below the throat.

Swallows spend a lot of time in flight as their main food is insects, caught as they fly, but they often settle on telegraph wires, especially before their migration in the autumn, when hundreds of them can be seen gathered together. The swallow's nest is saucer-shaped and made of pellets of mud and straw. It is generally in the rafters or on the beams in outhouses or sheds – the same bird may return to its nest for several years running. It lays four to six eggs between May and August and the eggs are white and narrow, spotted with brown. It has a twittering song when in flight, and a rather high metallic 'tweet'.

May Flower

Hawthorn

Mark the fair blooming of the hawthorn tree,
Who, finely clothed in a robe of white,
Fills full the wanton eye with May's delight.

Attributed to Chaucer

A Tortoise

A tortoise is a lovable pet that can fend for itself. When choosing one, make sure that his eyes are clear and that he is able to open his mouth.

He should live in a garden with both sun and shade. It is best to have a small area fenced off with wire-netting (about a foot high and firmly pegged to the ground) so that he can move about freely, but not escape. *Never* drill a hole in his shell as this is painful. He needs somewhere to shelter from extreme heat, perhaps a house made of a few bricks.

Tortoises are vegetarians: they love lettuce, cabbage, dandelion leaves, chickweed, clover; some also like tomatoes, fruit, and bread and milk. Sink the water saucer in the ground in the pen; in warm weather your tortoise will enjoy a bath in it too.

He will be ready to hibernate about October. He will become sleepy, and not want his food. Put him in a large box full of straw and keep it in a cold, but not frosty room. If you have fed him well through the summer, he will have stored enough to live on till spring. About March, you will hear rustling and know he is awake again. Give him a little warm water in a teaspoon – you may have to open his mouth for him. Let him wander in a warm room. After a few days you can put him in the garden in the day-time, but not at night if there are frosts.

Tortoises grow very tame; they will come out of their shells when called, and enjoy having their heads stroked.

Out of Doors

Country Lore

You will be out of doors most of the time from now on, so here are some things to remember about enjoying the countryside:

1. Shut farm gates if you find them shut, and leave open if you find them open.
2. Always climb over a gate at the hinge end.
3. Keep your dog on a lead if you are anywhere near sheep or cattle.
4. Do not leave bottles, tins, bags or papers lying about.
5. Unless you have permission, do not light any fires. If you do light a fire, keep it clear of all hay, straw or trees and pour water on it when you go away.
6. Do not pull up wild flowers by the roots.
7. Walk on the *same* side of the road as oncoming traffic.

Wild Flower Collections

You need a polythene bag, scissors, jam jar and water, newspaper or blotting paper, adhesive tape.

Some flowers, such as orchids, are rare and should not be picked. Take a book about wild flowers with you on your walks to look up the name of the flowers. Remember wild flowers droop very quickly so put them in a polythene bag as soon as you pick them.

May Out of Doors

Pressing and Mounting

1. When you return home put the flowers in water until you are ready to press them.
2. Take a sheet of blotting paper, flatten the flower and arrange the leaves so that alternate sides of them show.
3. Then, place more paper on top and press with a heavy book or box, and leave undisturbed for three days.
4. To mount, use plain paper and stick the flower firmly on to it in two or three places with adhesive tape. Be sure to write below it the date and place where you found it. Mount each flower on a separate page and keep them in a dry place as damp spoils pressed flowers.

Making Flower Pictures

Passe-partout, polythene, postcards or pieces of coloured card.

1. Arrange pressed flowers in a spray, using very little glue to stick them on the card.
2. Cover with polythene.
3. Bind round the edge with passe-partout.

Use them for Christmas cards this way or to make very small pictures for the dolls' house.

A Tree House

Everyone likes a secret place to escape to and play games or read in on a summer's afternoon. If you have a garden with four trees growing close together, and someone grown-up to help you, it is possible to make a tree house.

You need first four small blocks of wood. Nail these at the same height, one to each tree, not more than four feet from the ground. Place four long strong pieces of wood on these blocks and then firmly bind with rope or twine, making a square frame on the trees. On this frame place planks of wood, and nail them firmly in place.

A small rope ladder is the way up to the house and can be pulled up to keep 'the enemy at bay'. A basket on a rope is useful for hoisting up a picnic tea.

Daisy Chains

Pick daisies with long stalks.

1. Make a slit with your fingernail about ½ in. from the end of the stalk.
2. Thread a daisy through this slit.
3. Make a slit in its stalk and thread another daisy through this, continuing until you have made a chain as long as you want.
4. Then choose a daisy with a long, thick stalk, make a slit larger than the others and thread it very gently over the head of the first daisy.

Buttercup chains look pretty too.

Garden Bird Map

Birds like the blackbird, robin and thrush, usually live in 'territories' which they will defend in the spring-time. These territories often include part of a garden.

You will notice, if you look, that these birds prefer to sing from certain favourite places. These favourite places often mark the edges of their territory.

It is interesting to make a garden bird map. For this take two pieces of graph paper, one to draw the map from above (as the birds see it) and one for a side view (as you see it).

First draw in the outline of the garden using the squares on the paper to set the scale. You could make each small square equal to

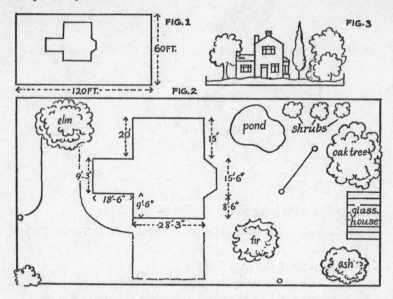

6 in. if you have a small garden, or equal to 1 yd if you have a large garden. Mark in the position and shape of your house – to make all the measurements use a piece of string about 10 ft long with a knot every foot. When you finish you should have a drawing which looks like Fig. 1.

Now go into the garden and measure the distances from the fences of all the trees, bushes, shrubs and posts where you know birds sit. Mark these on map (Fig. 2).

Watch the birds every day at the same time and then mark on the map which tree, post, or roof they sing from.

Draw the second map, this time imagining that you are looking from the house at both the back and the front of the garden. Mark the length of the garden, then see if the surface of the ground is even and mark this in (Fig. 3). This gives you a side view. Now measure the height of all the lower posts and shrubs and their distance from the house, and mark them in. Then fill in the places where they make nests and the favourite singing positions of the different birds – 'Blackbird in elm' and so on.

Things to Make and Do

Hobby Horse

You need broom handle, one old sock (dark colour), two buttons, needle, cotton, small piece of cardboard, length of tape, string, thick wool (light colour), and rags or newspaper for stuffing.

1. *The body.* Take a broom handle and saw it to make it as long as you are tall.
2. *The head.* Stuff the foot of an old sock with rags and tie a piece of string round the end, not too tight (Fig. 1).
3. *The eyes.* Sew two buttons on either side of the head.
4. *The ears.* Cut four triangles from pieces of rag in a colour to match your sock, and cut two pieces of card just a little smaller than the triangles (Fig. 2).
5. Take two pieces of rag, sew up the sides (BA and AC in Fig. 2) on the wrong side of the material, turn right way out, and slip in the triangle of card.
6. Fold in the raw edges, leaving enough material to sew them on to the head.

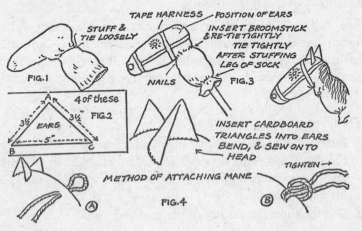

7. Fold B and C towards each other and stitch them on the head near the top.

8. *The bridle*. Tack one band of tape between the ears and eyes and another near the bottom of the head, and a short piece on each side to join the two bands (Fig. 3).

9. *The head*. Push the broom handle, sawn edge first, up to the string band and re-tie the string over the handle.

10. Pad round the handle inside the sock leg, bind with string and tie tightly (Fig. 3).

11. To make the head firm, put in two short nails, one under the 'neck' and one on the top by the last string binding.

12. Tie tape or string on each side of the nose band, fastening it at the end of the neck, and leaving a long loop to make reins.

13. *The mane*. Cut some thick, light coloured wool, into twelve-inch lengths.

14. Fold them in half, thread the loop through the neck, and thread the ends of the wool through the loop to keep it in place (Figs. 4a and b).

15. *Mouth, nose and eyes*. Outline in wool.

Decorating a Doll's House

You will need paint, wall-paper, brush, knife, sandpaper, paste, material, tape, elastic, needle, cotton, carpet, linoleum, Christmas cards, drawing-pins, cotton wool. People often re-decorate their houses in spring and may have some paint or paper left over which they will give you.

The Outside

1. Put the doll's house on a dust sheet and scrape off as much of the old paper and paint as possible with a scraper, knife or some sandpaper. Either repaint it or buy sheets of special brick paper for dolls' houses.

2. Cut the papers to the size of the roof and walls.

3. Mix some flour paste (p. 99) or buy a little paper-hanger's paste. Brush paste over the walls and roof.
4. Stick the paper on carefully, making sure it is the right way up, and smooth all the air bubbles out towards the edges of the paper with a clean, dry cloth.
5. When dry, you can paint the door and window frames.
6. Clean your paste brush with warm water and paint brush with turpentine *at once*. Otherwise they will dry hard and you will not be able to use them again.

The Inside

Decorate in the same way, but instead of painting the walls, paper them with wall-paper. If there is none to spare at home, a decorator's shop may let you have old books of wall-paper samples. If the rooms are small, you could cover the walls with pieces of material.

To Make Curtains

1. Cut a piece of material a little longer than the window and one and a half times the width.
2. Cut it in half and hem round the edges. Make a larger hem at the top and thread through a piece of tape or elastic. Fix this at the ends with drawing-pins.

To Make Bedclothes

1. Measure the length of the bed, and its width from the floor on one side to the floor on the other, allowing $\frac{1}{2}$ in. extra on each side for the hem.
2. Hem it neatly all round on the wrong side.
3. To make pillows (or cushions), take an oblong piece of material, fold it inside out and sew round the edge, leaving one side open for stuffing. Turn back to right side, fill with cotton wool and sew up.

For the Floors

If you have any old squares of thin carpet or linoleum, you could re-cover all the floors.

Pictures

Pictures can be made to hang on the walls. Use part of an old post-card or Christmas card. Cut out and edge with passe-partout and thread a piece of cotton underneath the passe-partout on the top of the picture, leaving about 2 in. each end to hang the picture from a small pin or drawing-pin.

Match-box Furniture

Chest of Drawers

You need six empty match-boxes, six brass paper-fasteners, glue, scraps of material or wall-paper, scissors.

1. Glue the match-boxes together in pairs, and then glue the pairs on top of each other (Fig. 1).
2. Pull out the trays and put on brass paper-fasteners for handles (Fig. 2).
3. Cut a piece of material or wall-paper long enough to cover the top and the two sides of the match-boxes. Glue in place, and trim the edges (Fig. 3). Leave to dry.

Table

You need one match-box tray, four used matches, small piece of thin material, scissors, glue.

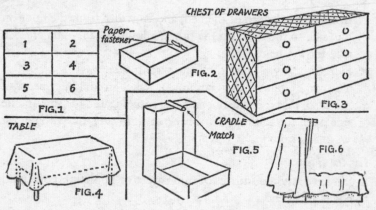

CHEST OF DRAWERS

1	2
3	4
5	6

FIG. 1

Paper-fastener

FIG. 2

FIG. 3

TABLE

FIG. 4

CRADLE
Match

FIG. 5

FIG. 6

1. Cut off the used ends of the matches, and make the four matches all the same length.
2. Glue the end of each match and stick one match into each corner of the inside of the tray. Allow to dry.
3. Cut a piece of thin material and place over the tray to make a cloth (Fig. 4).

Cradle

You need two match-box trays, one used match, small pieces of thin material, scissors, glue.

1. Glue match-box trays together at right angles and glue a match in centre of top tray (Fig. 5). Allow to dry.
2. Cut a piece of material long enough to drape over the match (Fig. 6) and down the sides.
3. Cut another piece of material as a cover for the lower tray.

Finger Painting

This is a lovely *messy* thing to do. And you can use the idea to make pictures for your dolls' house, or cards for birthdays, or even decorated wall-paper. You need flour, water, colouring, spoon, linoleum or brown paper.

1. Mix a fairly stiff paste with flour and water as follows:
   Put some sifted flour in a basin and make a hole in the centre. Add, slowly, enough cold water to make a thick cream, stirring hard all the time to avoid lumps.

N.B. If you need a stronger glue for other purposes, add more water to make a thinner cream, and then boil in a saucepan for a few minutes, stirring all the time until it thickens.

2. Colour it with powder paint.
3. Spread this over a piece of American cloth, linoleum or thick brown paper and make patterns on it with your fingers. It is easy to rub it smooth and start again.

Keep a bowl of water and towel near by to wash when you are too messy. You can also make patterns with spoon handles, forks and sticks.

Paper Houses

You need stiff paper, pencil, ruler, set-square, compass, paints, strong adhesive.

Try making a simple house from a single sheet of paper like the one in the diagram below. When you have mastered the idea you can try more elaborate buildings using the same method.

Take particular care to make the distance from the ridge of the roof to the eaves the same as that from the eaves to the gable peak, otherwise the roof will not fit the walls. These three points are indicated by 'a', 'b', and 'c' in the diagram and the dotted arc shows how you can measure them by putting the point of the compass on 'a' and drawing the arc 'b' to 'c'.

The doors are both the same size and the windows are all the same height and distance from the ground, so you should find it

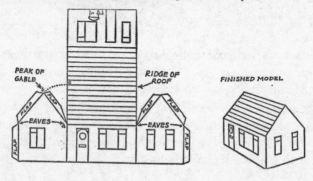

simple to draw these with your ruler and set-square, making some of the windows twice as wide as the others.

When you make your design do not forget to include the flaps as shown in the diagram. These are to be turned in and glued to the *inside* of the corresponding walls when you have folded the corners, eaves and roof-ridge of your building.

It is best to paint the house when it is folded and standing upright.

Try making a small village in this way with cottages of different sizes and a church.

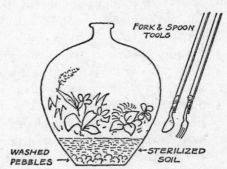

Bottle Garden

Select a large, balloon-shaped bottle, the kind that comes from wine merchants with cider or wine in it. Put an inch layer of small washed pebbles at the bottom of the bottle. Do this carefully by laying the bottle on its side so that it does not break. Then cover the pebbles with 3 or 4 in. of sterilized soil, bought from a gardening shop. The soil should be as dry as possible and you can use a paper funnel to pour it through; this will be easier and keep the sides of the bottle clean.

Make your own tools to work with. An old spoon or fork each tied to a long stick are effective ones. The most suitable plants to grow are those that like a humid atmosphere such as a begonia, a zebrina leaf plant or a maidenhair fern. You could have all three plants in the same bottle, and others, depending on the size of the bottle. Lower the plants into the bottle carefully, using your special tools, and plant them in the soil. Water thoroughly, making sure that all the soil is damp but not swimming in water. Put the cork in the bottle and the plants will keep damp and not need watering. Keep in a light place, but not in direct sunlight, and turn the bottle round occasionally. (It is *not* possible to grow plants from seed this way.)

Comb Pictures

You need sheets of white paper, cardboard, scissors, poster paints, large paint brush, cold water paste, old saucers.

1. Make your comb from stiff card about 8 in. by 2 in.
2. Cut out triangular wedges all the way along, about 1 in. in depth.
3. Put some paste into a saucer and mix with colour.
4. Paint this over the sheet of paper with your big brush, making sure that the paste is not too thin.
5. Starting at the top of the sheet, pull the comb over the paint-paste. You will see you have lighter lines left behind. You will soon discover various ways of making patterns by waving lines and weaving and crossing them. Then try using more colours, but always use a new comb for each colour.

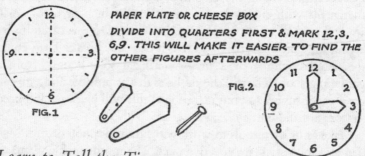

FIG. 1

PAPER PLATE OR CHEESE BOX

DIVIDE INTO QUARTERS FIRST & MARK 12, 3, 6, 9. THIS WILL MAKE IT EASIER TO FIND THE OTHER FIGURES AFTERWARDS

FIG. 2

Learn to Tell the Time

Make clock as in drawings above, using a brass paper-fastener to fix the hands. Remember every number represents 5 minutes. Learn to tell the quarter hours first: write them in above the numbers – 15 minutes past at No. 3, 30 past at No. 6 and 45 past at No. 9.

Sewing

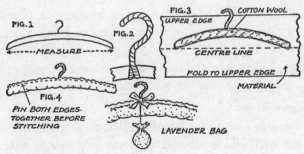

FIG.1 ···MEASURE···

FIG.2

FIG.3 UPPER EDGE COTTON WOOL

CENTRE LINE

FOLD TO UPPER EDGE

MATERIAL

FIG.4
PIN BOTH EDGES
TOGETHER BEFORE
STITCHING

LAVENDER BAG

Covering a Coat Hanger

You need a strip of pretty, soft material, coat hanger, cotton wool, one yard narrow ribbon or binding, scissors, needle and cotton, pin.

1. Cut a length of material about 6 in. longer than coat hanger and 6 in. wide.
2. Bind the hook with the ribbon. Starting at the top end, wind twice round in the same place before continuing. When you reach the wood, take the ribbon twice round from each side of the hook. Fasten end with a needle and cotton (Fig. 2).
3. Fold the material in half then fold tightly over the hanger to see that it will meet easily over the centre point (Fig. 3 : shapes of hangers vary so do this before you continue).
4. Lay the cotton wool thickly along one side of the hanger. Secure by winding a length of cotton round it. Repeat for other side.
5. Put the hanger on the centre line of the material, and bring the sides up over the top. Turn in the edges, pin in place close to the hook as shown in Fig. 4.
6. Fold in the ends and gather through both thicknesses with a long double thread. Work to the centre and fasten off strongly.

For a more special gift make a lavender bag (p. 149), and hang it over the hook.

Maypole Cake

You need a sponge sandwich (see p. 180), 3 oz. butter, 6 oz. sieved icing sugar, 2 dessertspoons of water or orange or lemon juice, coloured wool, knitting needle 10 in. long, packet of jelly babies. Beat the butter, icing sugar, and fruit juice or water until soft and spread half inside sponge, and the other half on top.

Maypole Decorations

1. Cut the wool in five 20-in. lengths. Hold them together so the ends are level, fold in half and tie a loose loop in the centre.
2. Slip the knitting needle through the loop and pull tight. Then push through the centre of the cake until it touches the plate.
3. Separate the strands evenly round the cake, bringing the ends to the edge and keep in place by pressing a jelly baby lightly into the icing on the end of each strand.

Jam Tarts

You need ½ lb. flour, ¼ lb. fat – either 4 oz. lard, or 2 oz. lard and 2 oz. margarine, salt, cold water, jam, pastry-board, rolling-pin, mixing bowl, pastry-cutter, tart-tins.

1. Set electric oven to 425°, gas to regulo 7.
2. Grease your tins with a little lard.
3. Sift the flour and salt into the bowl.
4. Add the fat, cut into small pieces and, using your fingers, rub into the flour until it becomes like fine breadcrumbs.
5. Add cold water, a little at a time, and mix to a firm dough. Be careful not to make your pastry too wet or it will be heavy.
6. Sprinkle pastry-board and rolling-pin with flour and roll out the pastry gently, away from you, until it is about ¼ in. thick.
7. Cut out the number of rounds you want, press carefully into the tins, and put a teaspoonful of jam into each.
8. Place on the top or second shelf of the oven for approximately 15 minutes, check after 10 minutes in case they are ready. Leave in tins until cold.

Pineapple Tops

Cut off the leafy top of the pineapple together with a little of the skin of the fruit and leave it to dry. After two or three days put it in some sandy soil. Water lightly. Keep it as warm as you can. Sometimes you will have to plant several tops before you have success, but when you have found one that forms roots (in about 2 weeks) re-pot it in some good sterilized soil. Keep damp and warm near light. The plant will not produce any pineapples but it makes a very pretty indoor plant.

Broad Beans Grown in Jam Jars

Soak some broad-bean seeds in water for a few hours until they swell. Cut and roll a piece of blotting paper and line a 1 lb. or 2 lb. jam jar up to the neck with it. About half way down, put the broad bean between the jar and the blotting paper. Pour about an inch of water into the jar and it will soak up to the top of the blotting paper. Always see that there is enough water to keep the blotting paper wet. It is possible to grow the bean in a warm light room, but it is quicker if you keep it in a dark cupboard until it germinates, then bring it into the light. Perhaps you would like to prepare two jars and keep one in the dark and the other in the light to see which grows the faster.

Outdoor Gardening

Tulips were first brought into England in the sixteenth century by travellers from the Near East, and Europe. If you have some in your garden, cut off the head as each flower dies, and when all are dead, lift the bulbs out of the ground with the stem and leaves still attached. Store somewhere dry for the summer months. Allow the foliage to die naturally as it will help build up the bulb for replanting in the autumn.

Seeds you can sow this month which will flower later on in the summer are: clarkia, candytuft, cornflowers and nasturtiums.

Games to Play

Here We Come Gathering Nuts in May

This game can be played by both girls and boys, indoors or out-doors. The children form two equal sides facing each other, with a line drawn between them or a handkerchief placed to show the centre. One side joins hands and walks up to the centre and back, singing:

> Here we come gathering nuts in May, nuts in May, nuts
> in May,
> Here we come gathering nuts in May, on a cold and frosty
> morning.

The other side then joins hands and walks up to the centre and back singing:

> Whom will you have for nuts in May, nuts in May, nuts
> in May,
> Whom will you have for nuts in May, on a cold and frosty
> morning?

Then the first side decides which member it will have from the opposite team and, advancing and retreating again, sing:

> We'll have — for nuts in May, nuts in May, nuts in May,
> We'll have — for nuts in May on a cold and frosty
> morning.

The other team then sings:

> And whom will you have to fetch him [her] away, fetch
> him away, fetch him away,
> And whom will you have to fetch him away on a cold and
> frosty morning?

The first side then decides on a child in their own line (if possible choosing one about the same size as the one from the other side) and sings:

> We'll send — to fetch him [her] away, etc., etc.

The two chosen members then have a tug-of-war with a handkerchief on the floor between them. The loser is the one who is pulled over the dividing line, and he joins the winner's team.

The game then begins again, this time the other side starting, and so on, alternating until one side has no players left – or until everyone is exhausted.

Find the Word

Any number of players, paper and pencil each.

One player chooses a long word like DISAPPOINTMENT, writes it down on a piece of paper and numbers each letter. Then he tells the other players how many letters the word has, so that they can make and number as many dashes on their paper.

Then he gives clues so that the others can work out his word. Look carefully at a long word and you will see it is often made up of other words. For example, from 'disappointment' can be made *sad, in, men, pin, paint,* etc. A few clues could be – giving the number of letters 8 and 9 – *the opposite of out*. The players will then write ――――――IN―――― on their paper. Next you might say 3, 4, 5, *the juice you find in a tree*, now you will have ――SAP――IN――――. Your next clue could be 1, 7, 13, *a short form of the name Donald*, D–SAP–OIN―――N– by which time someone has guessed the word and it will be his turn to choose a word.

Five Stones

If one day you have no companion, find five small pebbles and play five stones. It is one of the oldest games recorded – it was played by the Greeks – and you can play it anywhere. It is also called Knucklebones, as five evenly matched carpal bones were considered the best things to use, but five small pebbles or shells of a similar size will do. It has many variations.

One of these variations is played as follows: place the five pebbles in the palm of the hand, throw them up in the air, spread the fingers and catch them on the back of the hand. Practise by throwing up first one, then two, then three and so on, as it is quite difficult to catch all five at once.

Another variation is to place four pebbles on the ground, keeping one (A) to toss. Throw A up in the air, picking up one of the others with the same hand while pebble A is in the air, before you catch it again. Next time, pick up two at once while pebble A is in the air, then three and finally four. As you become more skilled, you can place the pebbles farther apart on the ground, or place another object to be picked up while all five stones are in the air.

I Spy

This is a very simple game which can be played by any number of players anywhere – indoors, outdoors, sitting, walking, or in a car. One player starts by saying 'I spy with my little eye something beginning with A' (or B, or whatever letter the word commences with) and the others have to guess what it is. The first to guess correctly chooses the next object.

Snap

Any number of players, one or more packs of playing cards or snap cards.

1. Deal the cards face downwards to each player until all are dealt. No player may look at his cards.
2. The player on the left of the dealer turns over the top card of his pile, placing it well in front of him face upwards on the table.
3. The player on his left plays his top card in a similar manner and each player round the table does the same until a card is turned up which matches one already face upwards. Whoever calls out 'Snap' first takes the cards and any others which are lying below them and places them underneath his unplayed pile. If a player calls 'Snap' in error his exposed cards are taken by the player whom he snapped. As players lose their cards they drop out, the winner being the one who finishes with all the cards.

Fancy Dress
Outfits

Pirates

You need a curtain ring (for an ear-ring), a striped jersey or tee shirt, trousers or jeans, wellington boots, small woollen cap, scarves, or cowboy hat, crêpe paper (any colour), an eye patch, cardigan, dagger or a sword.

Boots

1. To make large turn-down tops for your wellingtons, cut a piece of crêpe paper 9 in. deep, wide enough to fit in the top of your boot and stick it in with adhesive tape.
2. Turn the top of the paper down to make a flap, and stick the edges together.

Lapels and Cuffs

1. Cut wide lapels of coloured paper (black is very fierce looking) to wear over a cardigan.
2. Sew them on to the cardigan, so that the outside edge overlaps the stitches.
3. Make cuffs in the same way.

Hat

1. Tie a small bright scarf round your neck.
2. Tie another low over your forehead, tucking the loose flap under the knot at the back.
3. If you have a cowboy hat with a soft brim, stitch this in three places to make a tricorn hat to wear over the scarf.

Chefs or Cooks

(specially for very small children)

You need a small navy-and-white-striped apron, with black tapes at waist and neck, a white blouse or shirt, blue jeans, a clean white table-napkin (folded into a triangle, to be worn on the head, and tied behind the neck), a huge wooden spoon to carry.

Gipsies (Girls)

You need a blouse, a long cotton skirt over several layers of petticoats, brightly coloured apron, baby doll or small basket of heather or pegs, ear-rings, scarf round the head, no shoes, large shawl.

1. Tie the shawl across one shoulder to the opposite side of the waist.
2. Tuck the baby doll into the shawl.

Gipsies (Boys)

You need old shorts or jeans (if possible cut round the hem to look ragged), old striped jersey, ear-rings, stick to carry over the shoulder, with a bundle tied in a cotton scarf at the end of it, no shoes.

Clowns

You need a baggy pair of pyjama legs, gathered at ankles (non-striped material is best), patches of bright material, pyjama top or bright smock, white crêpe paper, tape, old hat, lipstick.

1. Sew on to the pyjama legs and top as many patches of brightly coloured material as you like.
2. Wear the smock over the top of the pyjama legs.
3. Cut the crêpe paper into six strips, 9 in. wide, 2 ft long.
4. Gather these strips on one side.
5. Sew them to a band of tape, which you tie round your neck.
6. Put an old hat on your head and give yourself a red nose and a big mouth with some lipstick.

June

The roses make the world so sweet,
The bees, the birds, have such a time,
There's such a light, and such a heat
And such a joy in June.

G. MacDonald

Midsummer's Day

June is the month of high summer. The month for roses, warm sun, tea in the garden and light evenings when it is hard to be early in bed. In all northern countries it is summer, but in the southern half of the world it is winter.

The 21 June is Midsummer's Day, the longest day in the year. Then the sun rises earlier and sets later than on any other day. It is also a day of magic, when fairies (if you believe in them) feast and dance from midnight to dawn.

Years ago people used to light bonfires on Midsummer's Day to encourage the sun to shine. They would hurl burning discs into the air and roll blazing wheels downhill in imitation of the sun's journey across the sky.

The great circle of stones at Stonehenge was built for the festival of the sun. At St Ives and Helston in Cornwall people still light fires on 21 June.

Yellow Hammer

The yellow hammer is found chiefly in hedgerows and is easily recognized by its bright colouring. The male bird grows brighter with age, and has a yellow head and underparts and chestnut upper parts, streaked with black except on the rump. The female is not so bright and has heavier markings on the head. The white tail feathers show when it flies.

It nests mainly under hedges and bushes. The nest is made of grass, moss, and hair. It lays three to five eggs, almost white but with purplish-brown scribbles on them, so that it is sometimes called the scribe bird. Its call is 'tink, tink, tink, tink tee', which sounds like the phrase, 'a little bit of bread and *no* cheese'.

June Flower

Ragged Robin

Where the river flows through woodland places, you will find the ragged robin.

It grows on a tall slender stalk, and has a pink flower with jagged petals veined with purple. Another name for it is the cuckoo-flower.

A Rabbit

A rabbit is a pet that is soft and cuddly, can live in a small space and is not expensive to feed, but you need to keep it outside the house. You can either buy a rabbit hutch or make one (with the help of a grown-up – see next page). It should be made of strong wood, be large enough for the rabbit to move about in comfortably, and have a wire mesh front to let in light and air. If possible make a small run of wire-netting next to the hutch so the rabbit can run about and eat the grass. Remember to peg it very firmly to the ground, as rabbits burrow. A water-proof hutch can be left outside all the year round but it is more comfortable for the rabbit if it is put in a shed or garage in bad weather.

Cover the floor of the hutch with straw and change it twice a week. Have two heavy bowls, one for water and one for food. In the morning, give your pet a bowl of mashed potatoes or potato peelings and scraps. Mix some bran into it as rabbits like food dry. In the evening give him lettuce, cabbage, or celery tops. In winter he will enjoy carrots or swedes.

Rabbits are rather timid, but if you handle them gently they become very tame and playful.

A Hutch for Small Animals

You need a packing case, nails, glue.

1. Remove the lid of the case and see that the walls and bottom are sound (Fig. 1).

2. Make a partition from a plywood sheet that fits across the box, put a hole in it for the animal to pass from one partition to the other. Climbing animals such as mice, rats and hamsters will manage with a hole high up in the wall if there is a suitable ledge or ladder provided for them to scale. Guinea-pigs, rabbits and hedgehogs will need a ground-floor opening.

3. Stiffen the plywood with thin battens at the front and back. Glue and nail the battens in position (Fig. 2).

4. Fix the whole partition in the desired place with nails driven through the sides of the case into the ends of the battens.

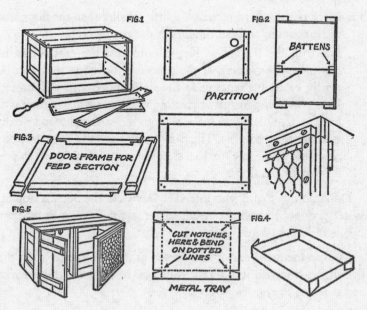

FIG.1

FIG.2

BATTENS

PARTITION

FIG.3

DOOR FRAME FOR FEED SECTION

FIG.5

CUT NOTCHES HERE & BEND ON DOTTED LINES

METAL TRAY

FIG.4

5. Make a frame for the door of the feeding section. Cover the front of it with a sheet of galvanized chicken wire-netting (with a maximum diameter of about ¾ in. across the holes) by screwing or nailing battens over the edges (Fig. 3). Be careful not to split the battens and frames. Oval nails help to avoid this.

6. Make a bedroom door from plywood stiffened with battens.

7. Fix the doors lightly in place with nails that are not fully driven home.

8. Screw hinges on to the doors at their outer edges (use a bradawl to prepare holes for the screws, or the wood will split when you drive them in).

9. When the hinges are in, remove the holding nails.

10. Make a catch for the doors with a hook and eye at the top of each door.

11. Trays can be formed from sheet aluminium or galvanized tin sheet. Cut out a piece about one inch too large for the floor space to be covered.

12. Mark within this a rectangle a little smaller than the floor area to be covered and cut notches at the corners (Fig. 4).

13. Bend up the flanges so formed and curl the tabs round to complete the corners. If the trays are too large they can be gently eased by tapping at the tight spots with a hammer. Don't be too vigorous or the tray will lose its shape. You will have no trouble if you make all your measurements and marks as accurate as possible. The flange may have to be cut away to clear the doorway to the sleeping compartment if this is flush with the floor.

Don't forget that if you intend to leave it in the open, a sloping water-proof cover must be arranged to carry rain water clear of the cage and its supports.

Measurements have not been given as it will depend upon the size of the case you use. Draw your box to scale on graph paper and mark in the doors.

Out of Doors

Flying a Kite

Kites have been flown for fun for thousands of years but they have also been used for more serious things. Long before balloons or aeroplanes were invented there are stories of kites carrying men into cities surrounded by an enemy, and being used to take supplies to people trapped on high mountains.

The gayest kites are made in China in all shapes, of fierce dragons, fishes, huge birds and strange human figures. Chinese children fly them at festivals like The Festival of the Moon.

A Paper Kite to Make

A kite is simply a flat surface held at a constant angle to the wind by a cord and a tail. The shape of the kite is not important, you can please yourself what yours looks like.

To make this one you need white or coloured stiff paper, 3 ft 6 in. length of $\frac{1}{4}$-in. square stripwood, plastic adhesive tape, thread, tissue paper, 100 ft length of light fishing line or string.

1. Cut the stripwood into one length of 1 ft 6 in. and one of 2 ft long.
2. Bind the shorter piece at right angles to the longer one 10 in. from its end (Fig. 1, overleaf).
3. Notch the ends of the stripwood (Fig. 2).
4. Stretch the thread lightly round the framework (Fig. 3) and tie the ends at one of the notches.
5. Lay the framework on the white paper, and allowing an extra 1 in. all round, draw the shape (Fig. 4).
6. Cut round this shape, notching the paper as in Fig. 4.
7. Fold the paper over the framework and secure all round with adhesive tape.
8. Make a tail with a length of thread 5 ft long, and tie a large bunch of tissue paper at the end (Fig. 5). Alternatively you can make an old-fashioned kite by attaching bunches of tissue

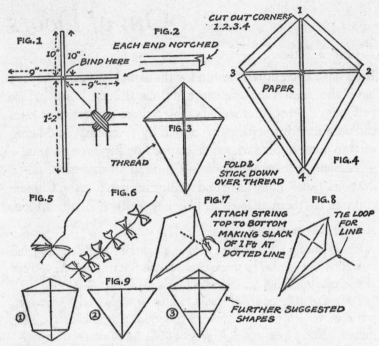

FIG. 1

FIG. 2
EACH END NOTCHED
BIND HERE

CUT OUT CORNERS
1.2.3.4

PAPER

FIG. 3

THREAD

FOLD &
STICK DOWN
OVER THREAD

FIG. 4

FIG. 5

FIG. 6

FIG. 7
ATTACH STRING
TOP TO BOTTOM
MAKING SLACK
OF 1 Ft AT
DOTTED LINE

FIG. 8
TIE LOOP
FOR LINE

FIG. 9

① ② ③

FURTHER SUGGESTED
SHAPES

paper to the thread, knotting them on at 6–9 in. intervals
(Fig. 6). Tie tail to base of frame.

9. Lastly, attach a length of thread or string to the top and
bottom of the longer piece of framework forming a loop 1 ft
in depth (Fig. 7). (Note: the paper surface should be on the
same side as the loop. Tie a knot in the loop 6 in. below the
crossing of the two members.) Attach your line to this loop.
(Fig. 8).

Take the kite out on the first windy day. If it does not fly steadily
with its nose pointing into the wind, add more tissue paper to the
tail. If it flies steadily, but without climbing, re-tie the knot further
towards the tail.

Once the kite is flying well you can experiment with shorter and
longer tails, and with different attachment points until you are
familiar with the principles by which a kite can be adjusted. Using

these principles you can design and construct your own kite and some suggested shapes are shown in Fig. 9.

Remember to keep the framework as light as possible, otherwise the kite will only fly in the strongest winds, and also, since it is only made of paper, it should not be flown in the rain.

Butterflies and Moths

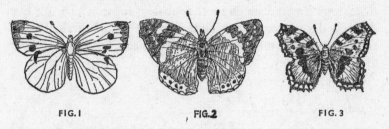

FIG. 1   FIG. 2   FIG. 3

From now until the autumn you will find plenty of butterflies and moths. They all belong to one big family of scaly-winged insects called Lepidoptera. Here are three guides to show you how to tell one from the other.

1. Butterflies have a 'knob' on the end of the antennae, while moths' feelers are usually straight.
2. Butterflies at rest raise their wings over their backs to an angle of 90° to the body, while moths usually fold their wings along their backs.
3. Butterflies fly by day and never by night, whereas moths normally fly by night.

Butterflies and moths lay their eggs on the special plant necessary for the growth of the grub. For example, the large white (Fig. 1) lays eggs on cabbage leaves. The clothes moth lays eggs on suitable clothing and carpets. She may lay hundreds of eggs or just a few.

The egg hatches into a caterpillar, the caterpillar becomes a chrysalis and from the chrysalis comes a butterfly or moth ready to start the cycle all over again.

Towards the end of autumn many butterflies and moths look for a warm place to hibernate. They may hang on the tops of curtains, behind bookshelves or in warm lofts. They sometimes wake up during the winter if there is a warm sunny day, but they seldom survive this early awakening. Hibernating butterflies, such as brimstone, peacock and small tortoiseshell (Fig. 2, previous page) are the first to be seen in the spring.

Most other butterflies die in autumn, but they leave behind them eggs, caterpillars or most probably pupae which can live through the winter. A few butterflies like red admirals (Fig. 3) and painted ladies migrate to warmer climates, but many of them die on the journey.

Collecting Grasses

Grasses are the most useful of all growing plants. Cattle, sheep and horses need them fresh and green, and also dried for winter feeding, but have you ever realized that wheat, oats, and barley, which are the basis of our own diet, are all kinds of grass? These are the most common farm crops you see. They flower during the summer, but will not actually be ripe enough for harvesting until the end of July, August or September, depending on the weather.

The flower-head of a grass is called an 'ear' or 'panicle' and the flowers it produces are called 'spikelets'. It is very difficult to identify grasses unless they are flowering. Below are the names of a few of the more common grasses.

Meadow foxtail. The panicle resembles a fox's tail and it is one of the earliest grasses to flower, from mid April onwards (Fig. 1).

Cock's foot. The panicle is made up of branches of all lengths, each one ending with a cluster of spikelets. It is in flower throughout the summer from May to October (Fig. 2).

Rye Grass. The panicle gives the impression of having been flattened, and the spikelets are arranged alternately up the stem. It flowers during June and July (Fig. 3).

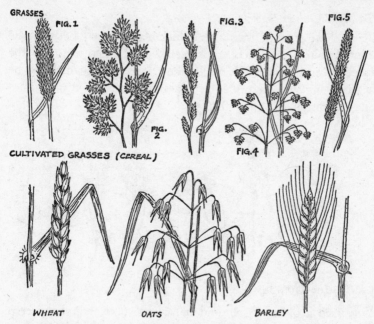

GRASSES

FIG. 1 FIG.3 FIG.5

FIG. 2

CULTIVATED GRASSES (*CEREAL*) FIG.4

WHEAT OATS BARLEY

Common quaking grass. The panicle quivers almost all the time. It is in flower during June and July (Fig. 4).

Timothy. The panicle resembles a cat's tail and this grass is often called common cat's tail. It flowers during the summer from mid July onwards (Fig. 5).

Games With Grasses and Plantains

Shooting Plantains

Plantains are not grasses, but are often found in lawns and on road-sides. You can make their heads fly as far as eight feet. Choose a plantain with a large head and thick stalk. Hold it with the left hand just below the head and bend the lower part of the stalk into a loop around the top part, just below the head. Hold tight with the left hand, pull the loop up sharply with the right, and the head will shoot off.

To Make Grasses Squeal

Pick a shiny piece of grass with a thick blade. Press it between the sides of your thumbs so that it is stretched tight. Blow through the space left in the centre. It will make a loud squeal which can be heard a long way off, a useful signal if you want to attract someone's attention.

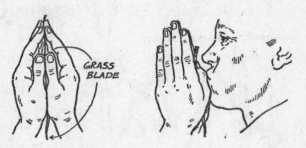

GRASS BLADE

Celluloid Boats

You need a piece of celluloid or acetate sheet, camphor, scrap balsa, tissue paper, bamboo, water-proof glue.

1. Take a piece of paper and cut out the shape shown (Fig. 1).
2. Trace the shape on to your celluloid with a pin.
3. Slip a small piece of camphor into the notch at the stern of your boat and launch it gently on the surface of a bowl of water. You will find that it will sail gently round until the camphor has dissolved.
4. You can now build a fleet of different boats, making the superstructure of balsa glued to the celluloid 'hull', and with bamboo slivers, pushed into the balsa, as masts and with tissue paper as sails.

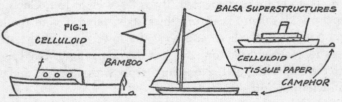

BALSA SUPERSTRUCTURES

FIG. 1
CELLULOID

BAMBOO

CELLULOID
TISSUE PAPER
CAMPHOR

Bubble Blowing

You need one polythene pot, a liquid detergent, water, a piece of flexible wire about 9 in. long.

1. Shape one end of the wire into a circle, the other into a loop for holding.
2. Put three dessertspoonsful of liquid soap and one of water into the pot.
3. Dip the circle of wire into this so that a film of liquid covers it and blow gently until a bubble floats away.

Rowing

Rowing is hard work, and you may find it best to sit by a friend and row with one oar each. Sit with your back to the front of the boat and the way you want to go, with an oar each side of the boat. To take a stroke, move your end of the oars forward so that the blades dip into the water behind you. Then pull the oars towards you, so that the blades pull through the water. Lift the blades out, and take another stroke. Look at the track of a rowing boat and the eddies will show where the blobs of water pulled by the oars are still moving through the water around them, while the boat has moved away in the opposite direction. If you use only one paddle or oar the boat will tend to turn round in circles, but you can stop this by paddling first one side, then the other.

Remember the wind will blow the boat about, and if there is a current you will be carried with it. Never set out in a boat unless you are certain you can manage the wind and currents. Rivers and tides are often too strong for anyone to row against, and it can be dangerous to be swept away by them. You should always wear a life jacket, especially if you cannot swim. If you do capsize, hold on to the boat and do not try to swim to land for it is easier for rescuers to see a boat than a swimmer.

E

Things to Do Indoors

Fans

Folding fans were first made in Japan. They were made of a circle of paper, sometimes pleated, pasted on to a light handle.

The fan was usually decorated or had verses written on it. In China and Japan it is still thought a favour to ask a guest or a friend to write a message on your fan.

Here is a fan for you to make. You need a strip of paper, scissors, glue, small stick.

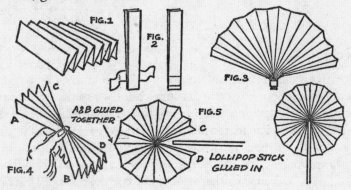

First Method:

1. Cut the paper to about 15 in. by 8 in.
2. Fold the paper like a concertina, making each pleat about ½ in. wide (Fig. 1).
3. Cut a narrow strip of paper about 1 in. wide and 4–6 in. long.
4. Glue this round the lower edge of the pleats to form a handle (Fig. 2).
5. Spread out the fan (Fig. 3).

Second Method:

1. Cut the paper to about 15 in. by 9 in.
2. Fold the paper as for the first type of fan.
3. Holding the pleats firmly in the centre (Fig. 4) spread the fan into a semi-circle.

4. Glue together the two halves of the top pleat.
5. Reverse the fan and complete the circle.
6. Glue the two halves of the final pleat halfway along the stick, which forms the handle (Fig. 5).

Decorating the Fans
While the fan is still folded in its concertina pleats, cut out different notches to make a pattern.

A Megaphone

You need a sheet of card, scissors, adhesive tape.
1. Put the card flat on the table and roll over one corner to form a cone shape.
2. Trim off the large point to make a complete circle at the wide end.
3. Stick a small piece of adhesive tape over the end to hold the card together, and bind round the cone.
4. Cut a small piece off the narrow end to make a mouthpiece. Call into the megaphone and it will carry your voice far away.

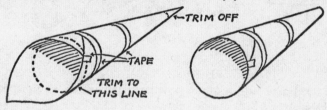

A Roundabout

You need one thick stiff card, one thinner card, a knitting needle, wooden if possible (No. 3), two cotton-reels, a tea plate 7 in. across, six small model farm horses, ruler, glue, modelling clay, poster paints.
1. Cut a circle of stiff cardboard using 7-in. plate as pattern, and mark the centre of the circle (to find the centre of a circle see p. 7). This is the platform of the roundabout.
2. Paint the card and reels a bright colour. Allow to dry, then put

the knitting-needle through one cotton-reel, then through a hole in the middle of the platform and through the second cotton-reel (Fig. 1).

3. Stick the six small model horses round the outer edge of the platform by putting their feet on little pellets of clay and pressing them firmly on to the platform (Fig. 2).

To Make a Gay Top for the Roundabout (using thin card):

Cut a circle 1 in. wider than the platform, and mark the centre. Draw lines from the centre like spokes in a wheel, with a pencil mark a scallop line between the drawn lines, cut neatly round it (Fig. 3) and colour. Turn down scalloped edge. Glue on.

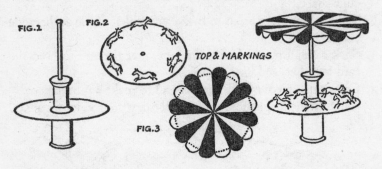

FIG.1   FIG.2   TOP & MARKINGS

FIG.3

Potato Printing

You need a potato, a knife, powder paint, water, newspaper to work on.

1. Cut a convenient chunk from the potato for use as a block, and carve a pattern into it. Use a very simple pattern as a potato is difficult to cut and impossible to use for complicated designs (Fig. 1).
2. Have paints mixed in saucers in the colours you wish to use.
3. With a small brush paint the potato block the colour you want.
4. Then, using the block as shown in Fig. 2 build up a rich pattern (Fig. 3).

OR use various very simple blocks to build up a picture (Fig. 4).

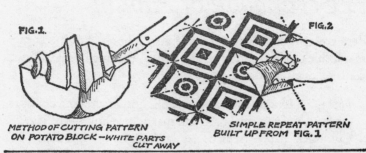

FIG.1.

FIG.2

METHOD OF CUTTING PATTERN
ON POTATO BLOCK—WHITE PARTS
CUT AWAY

SIMPLE REPEAT PATTERN
BUILT UP FROM FIG.1

BLOCK

FIG.3

SIMPLE REPEAT

HALF DROP REPEAT

USE SQUARED PAPER TO GUIDE YOU

VARY YOUR COLOURS SOMETIMES

FIG.4

USING VARIOUS SIMPLE SHAPES AT
RANDOM TO BUILD UP PICTURES

127

A Scrapbook or Album

Here are two easy ways to make a scrapbook. You need cardboard, thick paper, cotton-string, pencil, darning needle, scissors,
paints or cards for decorating.

1. *First Way*. If using a dress box cut off the sides. Make a line down
   the centre of the cardboard and make three holes – see Fig. 1.
2. Cut thick paper (which can be bought quite cheaply at a
   stationer) into sheets the same size as the cover. Place them on
   the cover.
3. Using a darning needle and several thicknesses of cotton-
   string, sew in-and-out of the three holes, finishing on the
   cover with a bow. See Fig. 2.
4. Fold over the cover, with the paper inside, and trim the edges
   to make them level.
5. Decorate the cover by drawing and painting a picture, or by
   sticking on Christmas cards.

SCRAPBOOK OR ALBUM (1)

FIG. 1   FIG. 2   FIG. 3

SCRAPBOOK OR ALBUM (2)

FIG. 4   FIG. 5

6. The contents of the album can be stuck in with glue, adhesive tape or corner hinges. Or slide the cards into ready-made slots. Do this very carefully; measure the card, then make two slits in the paper for each corner of the card – see Fig. 3. The cards can then be taken in and out and the information on the back easily read.

Second Way. For this you will need a hole puncher.

1. Cut two pieces of cardboard the same size, for the cover.
2. Punch two holes in exactly the same places in each piece of cardboard – see Fig. 4.

June Cooking

Jelly

You need a heat-proof basin or jug, hot and cold water, a packet of jelly.

1. Break the jelly into pieces and put them into a heat-proof dish which will hold one pint of liquid.
2. Cover the jelly with very hot water and stir gently until it dissolves.
3. Then add enough cold water to make a pint of liquid and leave in a cool place to set.
4. In hot weather it will take longer to set, so put it in a refrigerator if you have one, but remember to take it out a quarter of an hour before you eat if you want to enjoy the flavour.
5. Any fruit, such as oranges, bananas or raspberries, can be added to the jelly before it sets.

A Teddy Bear

If you can cast on and off, increase and decrease, and knit in garter stitch you will be able to make this teddy bear.

Abbreviations: K. = knit: sts. = stitches; inc. = increase; dec. = decrease; K. 2 tog. = knit 2 sts. together.

You need nearly 2 oz. double knitting wool, a pair No. 11 knitting-needles, stuffing, a little black wool, 2 buttons, ribbon.

Beginning With the Head: Cast on 17sts.

    1st and 2nd rows – knit.

    3rd row – inc. 1 st. at beginning and end of row.

    4th and 5th rows – knit.

    6th row – as 3rd row.

    7th and 8th rows – knit.

    9th row – as 3rd row (now 23 sts.).

    Next 10 rows – knit.

    2th row – K. 2 tog. K. to last 2sts. K. 2 tog.

    21st and 22nd row – knit.

    23rd row – as 20th row.

    24th and 25th row – knit.

    26th row – as 20th row.

    27th and 28th row – knit.

    29th row – as 20th row.

    Cast off these 15 sts.

    Knit another piece the same.

The Ears: Cast on 6 sts.

Next 3 rows – inc. 1 st. at beginning and end of each row (now 12 sts.).

    Next 6 rows – knit.

    Next row – K. 2 tog. six times.

    Cast off these 6 sts.

    Knit another piece the same.

The Body: Cast on 3 sts.

    1st row – knit.

2nd row – inc. 1 st. at beginning and end of row.

3rd row – knit.

Repeat 2nd and 3rd rows until there are 23 sts.

Next 20 rows – knit.

Shape for Shoulders and Neck: 1st. row – K. 2 tog. at beginning and end of row.

2nd row – knit.

Repeat these 2 rows until 13 sts. remain.

Cast off.

Knit another piece the same.

Arms: Cast on 14 sts.

Next 30 rows – knit.

31st row – K. 2, K. 2 tog., K. 2, K. 2 tog., K. 2, K. 2 tog., K. 2.

32nd row – K. 2, K. 2 tog., K. 2, K. 2 tog., K. 3.

33rd row – K. 2, K. 2 tog., K. 2, K. 2 tog., K. 1 (7 sts.)

34th row – knit.

Cast off.

Knit another piece the same.

Legs: Cast on 16 sts.

Next 32 rows – knit.

33rd row – K. 2, K. 2 tog., K. 2, K. 2 tog., K. 2, K. 2 tog., K. 1, K. 2 tog., K. 1.

34th row – K. 2, K. 2 tog., K. 2, K. 2 tog., K. 1, K. 2 tog., K. 1.

35th row – K. 2, K. 2 tog., K. 2, K. 2 tog., K. 1 (7 sts.).

36th row – knit.

Cast off.

Knit another piece the same.

To Make Up: Join the body, sewing together at outer edges, leaving an opening at the neck for stuffing. Stuff firmly, then sew up opening. Sew the legs and stuff them, then attach to the narrowest part of the body. Sew the arms, stuff them and attach them to the top of the body. Sew and stuff the head, and attach to top of the body. With black wool sew in a few stitches for nose and mouth. Sew on 2 buttons for eyes. Sew on ears to top of head. Stitch paws on arms and legs with black wool. Tie ribbon round neck.

Window Boxes

A vegetable box, hand drill, paint, wood preservative, stones.

Window boxes can be made at home from an old vegetable box, about 7 in. deep. Choose a sunny window sill and cut the box to fit its length. Paint the box a bright colour. Drill some holes in the bottom to allow any excess water to drain away, and then paint the inside with a wood preservative. Cover the bottom with small pieces of broken crockery or stones. Fill with a mixture of rich soil and leaf mould.

Sow grass seeds in the centre or on one side. This will divide the box and you can grow clusters of flowers each side. Trim the grass with scissors when it grows too long.

Outdoor Gardening

The lupin is a bushy plant with plenty of fan-shaped leaves and tall flower spikes which may be blue, pink, yellow, red, white or mauve. Not many years ago the only kind of lupin was a little purple wild flower, but a gardener called Russell bred the handsome plants you see now in gardens. Lupins can be grown from seed, but they do not flower until their second year.

Water the garden well this month. If there is not enough water to soak right down, the roots will grow upwards and shrivel in the hot sunshine.

Lettuces and radishes will be ready to eat now, and as lettuce seeds germinate in a few days it is as well to sow some each week in order to have a continual supply.

An Initialled Leaf

If you would like to have your initials on a growing leaf cut them out in black paper and stick them on a flat leaf. In the autumn remove the paper (you may have to soak it first) and your initials will appear. You can also initial your own special apple or pear, as long as you do it early enough, before the fruit begins to colour.

Indoors

Care of Cactus Plants

Cactus plants may flower this month and can be given a little water once a week if the weather is dry.

This is the time to take cuttings for new plants. Plant them, not too deeply, in sandy soil, and, if you can, keep them on a sunny window sill so that they have plenty of warmth.

Once the cutting has rooted and started to grow, plant it in ordinary cactus soil, which you can buy in small quantities from local gardening shops.

It is possible to keep most well-rooted plants outside on a sunny window sill for the next three months. The weather is usually warm enough and they will benefit from the summer rainfall.

Games to Play

Leap Frog

Leap frog is best played where it is soft to fall.

The fist player makes a 'back', that is he bends well forward, holds his legs with his hands, and tucks his head in.

Another player then takes a short run towards him, places his hands on his back and, with his legs wide apart, leaps over him. He runs a few yards farther ahead, and bends over to make another 'back'. Any number of players can join in, each making a 'back' after he has jumped over all the others.

Anyone who does not jump right over is out after three tries. The 'backs' must stand very firm and the jumper should only rest his hands lightly on them.

Changing Words

This is a game you can work out on your own, and puzzle your friends with later. Choose any word with four letters, and see if, by changing only one letter at a time, you can make it into something quite different. You will be surprised how many of these words you can work out, but remember you must make proper words at each step. For instance GAVE can become ROBS in this way: 1. GAVE 2. RAVE 3. ROVE 4. ROBE 5. ROBS. Or BOLD can become SAFE: 1. BOLD 2. SOLD 3. SOLE 4. SALE 5. SAFE.

You will be able to think of lots more.

July

Soon will the high Midsummer pomps come on,
Soon will the musk carnations break and swell,
Soon shall we have gold-dusted snapdragon,
Sweet-William with his homely cottage-smell
And stocks in fragrant blow.

Matthew Arnold, 'Thyrsis'

St Swithin's Day

July is named after Julius Caesar, the dictator of Rome, who was born in the seventh month, and who invaded Britain in 55 B.C.

The 15 July is St Swithin's Day.

> St Swithin's Day, if thou dost rain,
> For forty days it will remain.
> St Swithin's Day, if thou be fair,
> For forty days t'will rain nae mair.

St Swithin was Bishop of Winchester in the ninth century. He was a kind and humble man. When he died he asked to be buried outside his church so that his grave would be trodden on by the feet of passers-by, and would receive the raindrops from the eaves. The story is that when the monks wished to move his body many years later, it rained so hard for forty days that they gave up the idea.

The ceremony of swan-upping takes place in July. The swan-markers (wearing special uniforms) row up the Thames from London Bridge to Henley, collecting all the swans and marking the beaks of the cygnets.

Black-headed Gull

There are over forty different kinds of gulls. Although they are all essentially sea birds, gulls come a long way inland and breed on inland waters. The black-headed gull does this. It is one of the best known and smallest gulls in England. It has red feet and bill, pearl-grey back and wings. In the breeding season, its head becomes coffee-brown except for greyish-white feathers behind the eye.

It nests in colonies, amongst sand-hills by the sea, or on the marshes. It builds its nest of grasses, rushes or bracken. Towards the end of April it lays two to three eggs of an olive-green colour spotted with brown.

It eats mainly insects, but also earthworms, sand-eels, snails, mice and small birds.

It has a harsh call like a screech, the most usual notes sounding like 'Kwurp', 'Kwarr'.

July Flower

Red Campion

The red campion grows about two feet high and is found all over Britain in shady hedges and copses. In the summer it has deep-rose-coloured flowers which are pollinated by butterflies.

Goldfish

Goldfish are domesticated carp. Carp originally came from Persia, China and Malaya, they grow up to two feet long, become very tame and can live as long as forty years.

In their wild state goldfish are a dreary, dark green. A rich prince once imported thousands of goldfish to put in the lakes of his country. In these natural conditions, their gleaming gold scales became dull green again.

Kept in a tank or aquarium a goldfish is pretty and graceful to watch and easy to look after. Although he doesn't miss you when you go away, he does feel lonely for other goldfish, so provide him with as many companions as the size of the tank allows. Then they can all live a happy, fishy life together and will quickly become friendly and take food from your finger.

Bowls are not suitable homes as they do not have a large enough surface area of water to give sufficient oxygen. Choose a fish tank or aquarium and line the bottom of it with gravel, which you have first washed through with boiling water. Collect some water plants from a pond or buy them from a pet shop, plant these in the gravel, and then fill the tank with water. When the water clears, you can put in the fish.

Healthy goldfish will have fins that are upright and have *no* fungus on them. It is a common disease and you should remove such fish from the tank and change the water. Sometimes the fish can be cured by putting it in salt water and gently wiping off the fungus with a damp cloth.

Goldfish eat plants, dried food bought in packets, and, as a treat, live earthworms or flies. They must not be overfed. They need only a pinch of dried food each day. Uneaten food contaminates the water. Well looked after, goldfish live a long time.

Out of Doors

Fishing and Fishing Tackle

Fishing needs a lot of patience, but is splendid for anyone who enjoys being quiet and sometimes alone. Although if you want company you can make lots of friends amongst other fishermen. There are many different fish in the waterways and ponds of this country, each needing special types of rod and bait. The easiest way for beginners to start is by fishing for minnows. To do this you will need a flexible stick, a length of string, a worm, a jar of water from the stream.

1. Tie the string to one end of the stick, and the worm to the end of the string.
2. Sit quite still and dangle the worm in the water.
3. When you feel a gentle tug do not pull the line out immediately but wait a moment and then lift the stick upwards with a swinging motion to land the fish on the bank.
4. If you want the minnow for your aquarium, or to use as bait for larger fish, put it in the jar, otherwise, throw it straight back in the stream.

More Advanced Fishing

You need a rod (this need not be expensive), nylon line, a float, hooks of various sizes, a reel, some casts, splitshot, bait.

The Cast is a length of thin nylon or gut, which is attached to the end of a line. This is not so visible to the fish as the thicker line.

The Splitshot is a weight fixed near to the end of the cast to weigh down the line in the water. Beneath this is attached the *Hook*.

The Float is fixed to the line in such a position that the bait lies just off the bottom of the stream.

Bait. Fish don't all like the same type of bait, and as you become more experienced you will learn which type a particular fish prefers. Maggots, bought from an angling shop, are popular, but garden worms, house flies, stale bread, and lightly boiled potatoes can all be used.

Before you fish a stretch of water first find out if you need a licence or a ticket. These are usually obtained from the local angling club for about a shilling a day. Shops selling tackle will be able to tell you about fishing in the district.

Three of the first rules for fishermen are:

1. Never make a noise, since fish are easily frightened.
2. Try not to let your shadow fall across the water.
3. Always try to throw your line without making a big splash.

If you catch a pike, mind your fingers with its sharp teeth.

Never let a fish 'flap' to its death, always kill it by a sharp blow on the back of the head or, if you don't want it, put it back.

Binding a Rod

This is also useful if you want to lengthen a rod or stick, or make a new grip on a cricket bat.

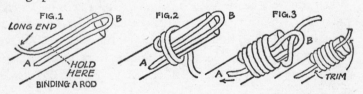

Camping

A Simple Tent

You need a square of canvas or heavy material, rope, tent pegs or pointed pieces of wood.

1. Tie the rope around the trunk of a tree and throw it over a low branch. Fasten the end to a tent peg and drive it firmly into the ground at an angle away from the tree (Fig. 1, below).
2. Fold the square of canvas in half diagonally to form a triangle and place it over the rope.
3. Peg down the three corners and add any necessary pegs along the sides (Fig. 2).

Try to choose a tree where you are able to put the entrance of the tent away from the direction of the wind. When you peg it down, make sure the material is well stretched or the rain will come through.

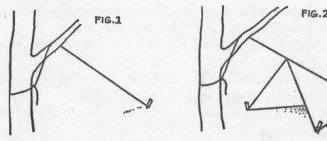

FIG. 1   FIG. 2

A Camp Fire

Making a camp fire is fun, but can be dangerous. You must remember these rules:

1. Clear all bracken, heather, grass and twigs from the space.
2. Collect small dead, dry twigs and some larger sticks.
3. Put a little straw or paper rolled into balls on to the space where the fire is to be laid, then pile on the twigs.
4. Light the paper and when it is alight put the sticks on the fire to make a cone shape (see above).

When the fire burns well put on logs, but keep it the same shape. When it is red hot you can start cooking. A good way to be sure a fire does not spread is to make a circle of large stones all round it.

Remember *never* to leave a camp fire until you are sure it is out. Use branches to beat it out, or pour water on it if nearly out.

Camp-fire Cooking

When you have got a good fire burning, you can think about food.

To Make Cowboy Dampers

You need 2 handfuls of self-raising flour, 2 teaspoonsful of baking powder, a pinch of salt, a knob of butter, some water.

Mix the flour, baking powder and salt together in a bowl, then add the water and make a dough.

Grease a frying-pan, heat it over the fire and, when hot, put in little cakes of the dough, about half an inch thick.

Cook first on one side, then on the other. When brown eat hot with butter and jam.

Baked Potatoes

These need to be done in the embers of a fire, so don't heap wood on the fire just before you want to bake potatoes.

1. Choose even-sized potatoes, not too large. Scrub and dry them.
2. Wrap them in damp brown paper, and push them into the embers.
3. Bake for half or three-quarters of an hour, according to size. When they are cooked they will feel soft if you press them.

Knots

Every girl and boy has to tie a knot some time. Here are a few useful ones (drawings are overleaf):

The Reef Knot

The best flat knot, will not slip, is easy to untie.

1. Hold an end of the string or rope in each hand, and put the right end across the left (Fig. 1).
2. Twist the right end once round the left, keeping the ends fairly long, then put the left *over* the right, passing the end through the loop (Fig. 2).
3. Pull the knot tight.

To undo, hold both lengths firmly and push towards each other.

An easy way to remember this is by saying to yourself 'Right over left and under, left over right and under'.

Slip Knot

Used to pull string or rope tight before securing.

1. Hold ends as before, but the left hand should hold the rope upright (Fig. 1).
2. Cross the right end over the left.

3. Loop this round the left string, pass the right end over the right length (Fig. 2).
4. Bring the right end up and under the cross of string and pass the right end back through the loop.
5. Holding both parts of right length pull tight.
6. The upright length will now pull easily through the knot.
7. Secure rope by tying a reef knot.

Clove Hitch

Used to fasten a rope to a post. Neither end will slip if pulled.

1. Pass the rope right round the post once so that the right rope crosses the left in front.
2. Now wind the right rope round the post again, holding the left-hand rope tight.
3. Bring the right rope round underneath.
4. Pass the right end through the last loop (marked X on Fig. 1).

The rope now looks like Fig. 2.

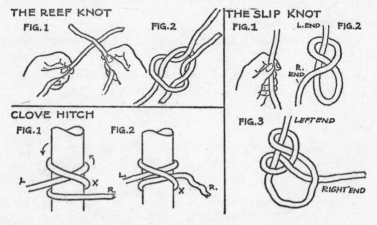

THE REEF KNOT — FIG. 1 — FIG. 2

THE SLIP KNOT — FIG. 1 — L. END — FIG. 2 — R. END — FIG. 3 — LEFT END — RIGHT END

CLOVE HITCH — FIG. 1 — FIG. 2 — L. — X — R. — L. — X — R.

Things to Do

Windmill Weathercock

You need a piece of stiff paper or thin card, paints, pencil and ruler, stout pin or small tack, length of thin wood or bamboo, cork.

1. Draw a square of eight inches on paper and draw lines four inches in length from corners. Cut these lines (Fig. 1).
2. Paint quarters in four colours. When dry turn over and paint colours in different order on back. Allow to dry.
3. Fold every other corner to centre and secure with a pin (Fig. 2). Fasten pin firmly into the stick, putting small cork between stick and windmill so windmill is free of stick and can spin easily.

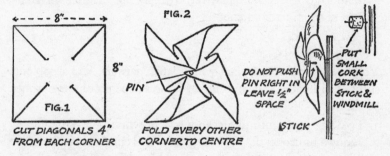

FIG. 2

←- - - 8" - - -→

8"

FIG. 1

PIN

CUT DIAGONALS 4"
FROM EACH CORNER

FOLD EVERY OTHER
CORNER TO CENTRE

DO NOT PUSH
PIN RIGHT IN
LEAVE ½"
SPACE

PUT
SMALL
CORK
BETWEEN
STICK &
WINDMILL

STICK

Original Postcards

Aunts, uncles, mothers, fathers and grandparents love to receive presents you make yourself. Make some postcards to send them. You will need blank postcards or sheets of cardboard cut to size, paints and brushes, glue, pencils and crayons, trimmings.

Here are some ideas for designs:

Material Pictures

Draw (or trace from a picture, seeing how to trace, p. 32) a man or woman, boy or girl, or all four. Dress them in felt, cotton, woollen material, coloured paper, lace or any scraps you can find, cut to the right shape and stick on the figures.

July Indoors

A Beach Scene

Draw a beach scene and colour it. Cover the beach with a layer of glue and sprinkle it with sand.

Leaf Picture

Take the skeleton of a leaf and glue it on a card. Using any number of leaves, make a pattern and colour it.

A Feather Picture

Collect some small feathers and with them design a picture, perhaps a bird on a palm tree.

Wood Shaving Picture

Cover the card with glue and sprinkle on the shavings. Tip off the surplus, and leave to dry. Paint them if you like – or arrange them to form a face or a flower, by brushing the glue on to the card in the form you choose.

Cut-out Figures

You need one sheet of plain white paper, scissors. Use an oblong sheet of stiff paper. The number of figures depends on the number of folds.

1. Fold the paper into pleats, about 1½ in. wide (Fig. 1).
2. Draw a figure on the top fold (Fig. 2) and cut round it carefully. Do not cut at the side edges. If you like, draw faces and clothes on the figures (Fig. 3), or dress them by cutting clothes as in Fig. 4 and hooking over the dolls' shoulders.

Arranging Flowers

When you start to arrange flowers look about you in the woods and fields and gardens and see how plants grow. Notice the various things that are natural to the surroundings in which they are growing: such as moss, ivy and stones, which you can often find wonderfully shaped and in strange colours.

You can use all these things in an arrangement; the only rule is to keep it simple so that everything shows.

Think about each thing and when you have studied carefully how and where it grows, then you will have a feeling for it and know how to use it.

Choose a plain vase or bowl to arrange the flowers in, and put some crumpled chicken wire in it so that the flowers will stand up. Remember that you can mix plants of different heights and sizes.

Collectors' Corner

Fruit Papers

You need a scrapbook, pencil and crayons, a map of the world (either traced or cut out of an old atlas), glue, scissors, fruit papers. This hobby helps you with your geography. Ask the greengrocer to leave some of the fruits you buy in their wrapping papers. Apples, oranges, lemons, grapefruit and tomatoes are the most common fruits to be wrapped, but you can also collect labels from melons and date boxes.

First trace a map of the world into the front of your scrapbook. Under the map draw a box for each kind of fruit, using a different colour for each one. Then, trim round labels before sticking them by the corners into your book.

Every wrapper will have a place name on it. Beside this name on the map put a small dot the same colour as the fruit. Throughout the year you will collect a list of countries which send fruit to England, and, if you also make a note of the month, the next year you will know when to look for the fruit you enjoy.

Make An Apron to Wear When You Cook

You need one yard of coloured material, needle, cotton, pins, scissors.

1. Cut a piece of material 36 in. by 4 in. for the band and ties, another 32 in. by 6 in. for the pockets, leaving a piece 32 in. by 30 in. for the apron (Fig. 1).

2. Take the apron piece and turn under, about half an inch, the edges of the two short and one long side, and then under again (Fig. 2).

3. Pin these folds and tack with large stitches, then hem neatly. Take out the tacking thread.

4. Run a gathering thread as straight as possible along the remaining edge ¾ in. below the top. Make sure the beginning is firmly stitched and then, with a running stitch, sew to the end (Fig. 3). Do not finish off but pull the thread, so that the material gathers, until it measures 18 in., and then finish off firmly.

5. Place the band right side down on the gathers, ¼ in. from the top (making sure the centre of the band is over the centre of the

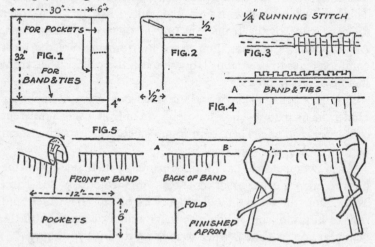

apron), tack in place, and sew firmly from A to B with running stitches (Fig. 4). Fold the band over the top of the gathers and turn edges under as in Fig. 5. Pin in place and hem the back of the band from A to B.

6. Sew the two long ends of the band together with a neat running or overstitch, turning the edges under first. These are the ties.

7. Finally, cut and sew on pockets. From the strip 32 in. by 6 in. cut two 12-in. lengths. Fold these in half (see drawing) with the fold at top, turn all edges to the inside. Press with a warm iron. Pin on to the apron and hem round three sides.

Lavender Bags

Cut the lavender flowers from the bushes before they are fully open (usually in early July). Spread the flowers on sheets of paper and leave them in a warm room to dry. For the bags you need small scraps of fine muslin or nylon material, cotton, needle, scissors, ribbon or narrow edging lace, paper, pencil, warm iron.

1. Cut a paper pattern 4½ in. square. Pin the pattern on the material and cut out two pieces.

2. Oversew the seams leaving a 1½-in. opening along the selvedge side to put in the lavender. Turn the bag inside out and press flat with a warm iron. The bag will now be 4 in. square.

3. Stitch on lace for decoration. Fill the bag with the dried lavender. Stitch up the opening.

The scent from the lavender will last for months, so these bags will keep for Christmas presents.

To grow your own lavender buy a small bush and plant it in September or March.

Here are some shapes you can make:

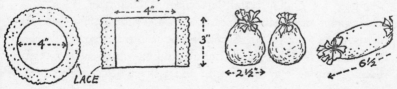

Cold Drinks for a Hot Day

To make a pint of *Lemonade* you need four lemons, four table-spoons of caster sugar, water.

1. Squeeze the lemons and pour the juice into a pint jug.
2. Add the sugar and enough boiling water to dissolve it. Fill the jug with cold water and put in refrigerator.
   A delicious variation is half orange and half lemon.

Fruit added to ready-made squash or homemade lemonade improves the look and taste of it. Add any of the following: strawberries, raspberries, stoned and halved cherries, a sliver of lemon peel, slices of orange or lemon, a thin slice of cucumber peel. A few washed mint leaves can be added when you take the jug out of the ice box, where it must have been for *at least* an hour before you drink it.

Iced Chocolate

You need cocoa, hot milk, cold milk, sugar.

Mix the cocoa and sugar with hot milk, then fill the jug with cold milk and allow to stand. A pinch of powdered coffee, added when mixing, improves the drink.

Iced Coffee

You need four tablespoons coffee, boiling water, sugar.

Make a small amount of very strong coffee. For one pint use four tablespoons of coffee. Pour half a pint of boiling water on to the grains. Add sugar. Stir well and leave for half an hour to settle. Strain into a pint jug, put into the refrigerator; later add iced milk to taste.

Iced Tea

You need tea, boiling water, lemon, mint, cucumber, sugar.

Make China or Indian tea, not too strong, with boiling water in the usual way (see p. 18). Strain and pour into a large jug. When cool put into the refrigerator. Before drinking add to each pint two slices of lemon, a sprig of mint and a sliver of cucumber peel.

Sandwiches

The easiest way to make sandwiches is to use a sliced loaf of bread. Fresh bread is difficult to cut and stale bread is not appetizing. Butter each slice of bread on one side and prepare the fillings. Here are a few suggestions for them:

1. Hard boil an egg. When cool, peel and mash with a fork adding a little salad cream, salt and pepper.
2. Ham, pork luncheon meat, liver sausage or corned beef, topped with slices of tomato.
3. Marmite, spread very thinly, covered with shredded lettuce or chopped watercress.
4. Tinned sardines, crab meat, tuna fish or salmon mashed and mixed with salad cream. These are best with brown bread.
5. Cream cheese, topped with a little chopped chives. Some people enjoy cream cheese and date sandwiches or cream cheese and strawberry jam.
6. Tomatoes, skinned, cut in slices, seasoned with salt and pepper and covered with chopped parsley.
7. Fish or meat paste, jam, honey or marmalade.
8. Bananas, thinly sliced, make delicious sandwiches but these must be made just before eating as bananas turn black if left. They can also be mashed.
9. Peel, core and slice an apple and mix with chopped dates.

Another, more interesting way, is to buy a long 'tin' loaf and cut it into about eight long slices *the wrong way*. Then butter and put a different kind of filling all along each of these long slices. Put them on top of each other, press down with something heavy and put in the refrigerator.

When the loaf is cold and stuck tightly together slice downwards as if you were cutting ordinary slices. Then you'll have sandwiches with different flavours in each.

Outdoors

Weeding the Garden

Weeds choke flowers and they die. So, if you want flowers to grow in your garden you must keep it free from weeds. Plants grow fastest in the spring and early summer and it is then that you are kept busiest pulling out the weeds.

Sometimes it is difficult to tell weeds from cultivated plants. Here, to help you decide which are which, are twelve of the commonest weeds. Be ruthless, even though some of them look as pretty as flowers.

Dandelion, plantain (has brown heads), buttercup, poppy (everyone knows these), creeping thistle (has mauve flowers), chickweed (little white flowers), nettle, scarlet pimpernel (star-shaped red flowers), sowthistle, daisy, speedwell, and bindweed (has small white trumpets).

Be sure to take up the whole root of the weed, as, if you leave any small bits behind, it will grow again. Use a small hand-fork and loosen the soil around the root until you can raise the plant from the ground without breaking off the roots. Shake off any loose soil and gather the weeds into a pile to throw away.

Saving Seeds

If you save seeds from plants your gardening will cost less. Make a collection of seeds in small envelopes and be careful to mark each with its name and colour, and keep in a cool, dry place.

Some seeds can be collected by knocking the plant and letting the seeds fall into your hand, others will not fall out unless they are quite dry. To gather these you must pick the flower and hang it upside down by the stalk for a few days.

Useful Hint

As flowers die, if you cut off the dead head with a pair of scissors, it will help to keep your garden tidy and the greenfly away.

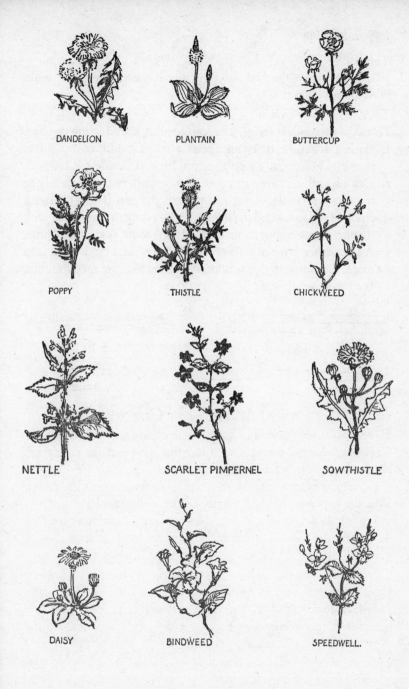

DANDELION

PLANTAIN

BUTTERCUP

POPPY

THISTLE

CHICKWEED

NETTLE

SCARLET PIMPERNEL

SOWTHISTLE

DAISY

BINDWEED

SPEEDWELL.

Tidy Paths

When you have finished weeding the garden, sweep the paths with a twig broom.

To Make a Twig Broom

To make this collect twigs, a broom handle, tarred string or cord.

1. Gather a bundle of twigs about 3 ft long and as straight as possible. Have ready a pole, or old broom handle 4 ft long.
2. Cut a length of tarred string or strong cord, and tie it firmly to the broom handle, about 12 in. from the end (Fig. 2). Place a circle of twigs around the handle and bind them into place with string. Allow about 12 in. of the twigs to lie along the handle.
3. Add another layer of twigs on top of these and bind them into place. Continue in this way until all the twigs are used, binding the top layer on very firmly (Fig. 3).

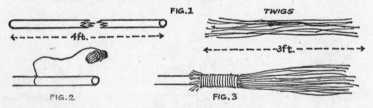

FIG. 1 TWIGS ←– – – – 4ft. – – – –→ ←– – – – –3ft.– – – – –→ FIG. 2 FIG. 3

Indoor Gardening: Mustard and Cress

Have ready two packets of seeds – one of mustard and one cress. Cress takes longer than mustard to grow, so plant the cress seeds about three days before the mustard seeds.

Cover the bottom of a large saucer with double blotting paper. Wet the paper with water and shake the seeds over it.

Leave the saucer in a warm, dark cupboard and water it every day until the seeds germinate. Once the mustard and cress is growing bring it into a warm room until it is ready to cut.

Cress Hog. If you can make a clay cress hog in your school pottery class, it is a nice way to grow cress. The hog must not be glazed.

Soak it for an hour in water and soak the cress seeds for a few minutes. Then arrange the seeds over the hog's back and fill the centre with water. Proceed as above.

Games to Play

French Cricket

You need a bat, or flat piece of wood or *old* tennis racket, ball, two or more players.

This is a fine game to play in gardens, parks, fields, or on beaches.

The object of the game is to stop the bowler from hitting your legs below the knees. The bat may be held anywhere round the legs. Should the ball hit your legs, you are out, or if you give a catch to one of the other players you are out. You are allowed to turn round only when one of the players has not got the ball.

Runs are scored by passing the bat round your body, changing it from hand to hand behind your back, each round counting as one run.

Plant Quiz

One person selects a number of trees, shrubs, flowers and grasses and ties a small card, with a number on it, to each of them.

The rest of the party are then given pencils and paper and must go round writing the names of the plants against the matching number on their paper. The winner is the one with the most correct answers.

French 'He'

A game for any number of players.

The player chosen to be 'He' must catch one of the other players by touching him on some part of the body. The player caught must then put his hand on the part touched, and keep it there until he has managed to touch another player. If touched on the foot, a player must hop after the others.

Chain 'He'

A game for any number of players.

The player chosen to be 'He' runs after the other players. As soon as he catches one, the second player links arms with the first and they run together to catch a third. The third then links arms and the three must run together after the others until one only player remains free. The last player to be caught is the winner of the game.

Old Maid – *for wet days*

Any number of players, a pack of cards.

Special packs of cards are made for this game, but it can also be played with an ordinary pack of playing cards, the rules being the same.

The Queen of Spades is taken out of a pack and put away, leaving fifty-one cards which are dealt out to the players. Each player looks at his cards and matches any pairs he may have in his hand, e.g. two eights, two tens or two kings, and puts them face downwards on the table.

The player on the left of the dealer then offers his cards to his left-hand neighbour, holding them face downwards in the shape of a fan. His neighbour selects one and, if it pairs with a card in his hand, puts the pair down. He in turn offers his cards to the neighbour on his left in the same way and the process is repeated until all the cards are paired except one. The player left with the odd card is the 'Old Maid'.

Where Go The Boats?

Dark brown is the river,
  Golden is the sand.
It flows along for ever,
  With trees on either hand.

Green leaves a-floating,
  Castles of the foam,
Boats of mine a-boating –
  Where will all come home?

Robert Louis Stevenson

Lammas Day

August is the month when school is closed and families pack up and go away on holiday. Off they go in all directions by car, by train, by bus, by foot, by steamer and by aeroplane, to the sea, the country or to strange lands.

It is the time for doing what you like, for buckets and spades on the beach, for sailing and fishing, for picnics and birdwatching.

Like July, August was called after a Roman, Augustus Caesar, who as well as giving it his name, increased the number of its days from thirty to thirty-one.

The harvest ripens in August and the crops are gathered. In the early English Church 1 August, Lammas Day, was the beginning of the harvest festival, when loaves of bread were made from the earliest ripe corn and taken to the church to be consecrated.

Once, before the days of mechanical reapers and binders, farmers used to give their farm workers a present of a pair of gloves on Lammas Day to protect their hands against the thorns and thistles growing amongst the crops they would soon be gathering.

The Oyster Catcher

The oyster catcher eats mussels, cockles and periwinkles; when there are not enough of these it makes up with whelks, shrimps, earthworms, insects and holothurians (sea-slugs and sea-cucumbers). It has a long, straight, orange-red bill, black-and-white plumage, and pink feet. Its nest may be a hollow in sandhills, on shingle or mudflats, or amongst rocks.

At the end of April or early in May it lays usually three yellowish eggs spotted and streaked with black. It has a loud, shrill call, 'kwick, kwick', and, when frightened, a call sounding something like 'heep-a'.

Scarlet Poppy

There is an old proverb that says: 'Ill weeds grow apace', which in the case of the scarlet poppy is very true, for one single poppy head holds 50,000 seeds. This is why, despite its prettiness, farmers do not like it, for it grows with corn.

In France the scarlet poppy is cultivated for the oil in its seeds which is used in cooking. In England there are four types. It has many country names such as *cheesebowl* and *headache*, and all poppies have a scent which encourages sleep.

A Grass Snake

In Britain there are only three snakes: the adder, the smooth snake, and the grass snake, which is the commonest. It lives in open woodland country and in hedgerows. There are several colour varieties, but in England it is greyish-coloured, usually with black spots or narrow crossbars on the back and vertical ones on the flank; it has an orange or yellow collar on the neck, bordered behind with black. Males seldom grow longer than three feet, females grow larger. It is fond of water and is a good swimmer. It does not bite when it is caught and soon becomes tame in captivity and, if properly looked after, lives for several years. Its main food is frogs but it also eats toads, newts and fish.

It lays eggs in June, July and early August and its young hatch two months later.

Slow Worms

Slow worms look like snakes but are legless lizards and have eyelids. Like most lizards they have fragile tails which will fall off if roughly handled. These do grow again but never as long as before.

Slow worms enjoy sunbathing on fine days, but if you are looking for one you are most likely to find it under stones or logs in woods, heaths and in gardens. The grown-up slow worm is brown, sometimes with darker stripes and sometimes with blue spots. They are easy to catch, do not bite, and mainly eat worms and slugs.

The young are born alive in September and are very beautiful. They are black with lengthwise gold or yellow stripes.

For August Travellers

Train or car journeys sometimes seem terribly long if you cannot think of anything to do. Here are a few ideas:

Things to do in the Train

Check the Speed

This only needs a watch with a second hand and the ability to do a little arithmetical division. If you look out of a train window you will see at regular intervals what look like little two-armed signposts set beside the track. The arms have numbers on them and are at different angles.

The posts are actually at $\frac{1}{4}$-mile intervals and indicate the slope of the track to the train driver. If you note from your watch the number of seconds it takes to travel from one signpost to the next you have obviously found out how long it takes the train to travel a quarter of a mile. By dividing this number of seconds into 900 you can then work out the speed of your train in miles per hour.

> i.e. Let x be the number of seconds it takes the train to cover the distance between two consecutive posts.
>
> x seconds for $\frac{1}{4}$ mile $= 4x$ seconds for 1 mile.
>
> There are 3,600 seconds in an hour.
>
> Therefore miles covered in 1 hour (i.e. speed of train)
>
> $$= \frac{3600}{4x} \text{ m.p.h.} = \frac{900}{x} \text{ m.p.h.}$$

White Horse

Make a list of not too common objects that you could see from the train, e.g. a white horse, a red-haired person, a boy with a pack on his back, a steeple with a weather cock. Whoever calls out first when he sees one of these scores a point. This game is equally good for playing in a car, but you will probably need to make a different list of things to look out for.

For August Travellers

Word into Sentence

Each player is given the same long word, and is told to use its letters in their right order as the opening letters of the words in a sentence. CHANGELING could become Chew Haggis And Never Grumble, Everyone Likes it, Nobody's Glum.

Constantinople

Choose a long word, and set a time limit of five or ten minutes in which each player writes down as many words as he can make out of its letters. Each word must have at least three letters, and must not be a proper name or slang. At the end of the time limit, count up the words you have made, and see who has thought of the most.

Shopkeeper

Pick out a story in a newspaper or magazine, and cross out all the nouns. Some serious piece of writing will produce the funniest results.

Say to your companion, 'You are a shopkeeper. What kind of shop do you keep?' and he tells you perhaps that he is a grocer or an ironmonger. Then you read out the story. Every time you come to one of the words you have crossed out, you wait for the shopkeeper to fill the gap with the name of something he sells in his shop.

Things to do in the Car

If you travel by car you will probably see more interesting things than from a train, as you will go right through the middle of some towns.

Inn Signs

Make lists of the names of the inns you pass, and see which have the best signs. You might have a competition between the people sitting on one side of the car and those on the other, to count whether the left or right side sees more signs. Or see

162

if you can go through the alphabet with inn names beginning with the right letter, e.g. The Antelope, The Bear, The Castle.

A Surprise Basket

Persuade your mother to make up a surprise basket for you, but don't wait to ask her until the day before you leave or she will be too busy. Into the basket she will put some small surprise packets to be opened at half-hourly intervals. Inside there might be a coloured pencil, potty putty, a padlock and key, a little puzzle, or something to read.

The Highway Code

Have a copy of this in the car with you, and ask each other questions from it. It sounds easy, but you will be surprised, for instance, how many people do not know the order of the colour changes in traffic lights.

A Chain Story

This is the story-telling game they played in *Little Women*. One person starts telling a story, as exciting as possible, and breaks off in the middle of an episode. Either the next person in a clockwise direction must go on with the story, or someone the first story-teller chooses. When the second story-teller has had a turn, he stops suddenly to let someone else continue.

First Aid

Be the person the family turns to in emergencies. Make a first-aid box for holidays – it should have gauze, gauze bandage, adhesive dressings, a roll of 1-in. adhesive tape, cotton wool, antiseptic, petroleum jelly, calamine lotion, baking soda, scissors, tweezers, needles, matches, thermometer.

Look over the page to see how you use them:

Animal Bites

Wash the wound at once under running tap water to wash out the animal's saliva. Then bathe it for five minutes with gauze and plenty of clean water. Rinse with more water and cover with a dressing. See a doctor immediately.

Ant and Mosquito Bites

Wash the bites with soap and water and put on them a paste made of baking soda and a little water, or use calamine lotion. If there is a swelling cover with a cold-water bandage.

Blisters

Try not to break the skin as it is the best protection against infection. But if the blister has to be broken first wash with mild antiseptic solution then sterilize a needle in the flame of a match, puncture the blister near the edge and press gently to drain off the fluid. Cover with a dressing.

Bruises

Place a cold compress (cotton wool or a towel soaked in cold water and wrung out) over the bruise.

Minor Burns and Scalds

Wash your hands thoroughly before treating the burn. Then run cold tap water over the burn to ease the pain. If the skin is not blistered put on petroleum jelly and cover with several layers of sterile dressings. If the skin is blistered just apply dressings and keep out the air. Don't apply ointment, oil or antiseptic. If the burn is large see a doctor.

Cuts and Scratches

Always wash your hands thoroughly before treating any wound. Wash the skin round the wound with soap and running tap water. Wash away from and not towards the wound. When the surrounding skin is clean wash the wound with soap and running tap water, using fresh sterile gauze. Put mild antiseptic on the wound and when it is dry cover with sterile gauze and a bandage.

Something in the Eye

Close both eyes for a few minutes. If this has not dis-lodged the object, hold the lashes of the upper lid and pull it out and down over the lower lid. If that doesn't succeed bathe the eye with an eyebath.

Hiccups

Take a deep breath and hold it as long as you can. Slowly sip several glasses of cold water.

Nose Bleed

Sit quietly with head bent forward and press nostrils together for five minutes, or lie down with a cold wet towel across the face.

Splinters

Wash round the splinter with soap and water. Sterilize a needle and tweezers by boiling them for five minutes. Loosen the skin round the splinter with the needle and then remove it with the tweezers. Cover with a dressing.

Wasp and Bee Stings

Remove the sting if visible. Run cold water over the sting to ease the pain. Bathe in water in which baking soda has been dissolved, leave on a wet bandage of the same.

Sunburn

If the skin is red but not blistered pat on calamine lotion very freely. If there are blisters or the burning is severe make a weak solution of baking soda (two tablespoonsful of soda to one quart of water), wet a sterile dressing with it, and put on the burn. Do not use anything greasy and don't expose skin to the sun until burn is healed.

Sunstroke

Rest in a shaded place or darkened room with cold towels on the head.

On the Beach

If there is a small stream running on to the beach make elaborate dams and waterways. If there is no stream, make rivers and dams from one rock pool to another.

Collecting Seaweeds

The best time to find seaweeds is at low-water on the three days before and after new moons. Then tides flow higher and ebb lower than at other times. The best place to find seaweeds is where rocks run out to sea, scattered about rocks on the beach, and at the foot of cliffs washed by the sea.

Seaweeds grow in three levels on the shore. Highest up the beach are the green seaweeds. These are exposed to the air at all low tides. Next, between high- and low-water level, are the brown seaweeds. The red seaweeds grow in deeper water and are not usually uncovered.

Sea-lettuces are green seaweeds and have flat, wide fronds. The most common brown seaweed is the bladderwrack; it has flat, forked branches with round air-bladders on either side which hold up the plant when it is floating in water.

The yellow-brown oarweeds or tangleweeds are uncovered only at the lowest spring tides, but sometimes can be picked up on the beach after a gale.

Red seaweeds are also found sometimes. Their colour is due to a red pigment, which in the light becomes redder.

When you have collected the seaweeds wash them in salt water and dry them on a soft towel before pressing them. Then lay them on a piece of muslin between two sheets of blotting paper and put several layers of newspaper on each side of the blotting paper. Place this under a heavy weight and leave for several days. When the seaweeds are quite flat and dry, mount them in a book by putting a piece of adhesive tape over the stalk. Look up the name in your reference book and write it underneath, with the date when you found it and the place where it was growing.

Sand Games – to Play Alone

Beachcombing
If you can be first along the high-tide line in the morning, especially after a strong on-shore wind, you will often find many exciting treasures.

Ducks and Drakes
This can be played on any calm stretch of water. Find some flat stones from 1 in. to 4 in. across and rest them horizontally on your hand with the first finger around the edge of the stone. With a flicking movement of the wrist send them flat across the water and see how many times you can make them jump on the surface. With a good stone and a clever throw you will often get ten to a dozen jumps.

Angels in the Sand
Lie flat on your back on the sand and move your arms up and down from your sides to above your head. Move your legs sideways as far as you can, and when you stand up, you will find you have left an imprint which resembles an angel.

Collecting Sea Shells

Some of the most common shells are whelks, fan shells, limpets, cockles, mussels, top shells, piddocks, oysters, winkles and slipper shells. Try to find as many varieties as possible to start a collection and for making presents.

Keep the shells in cotton wool in small cardboard boxes, with the name of each shell written on the box, or mount them on a sheet of stiff black paper. Pin the paper to a board with drawing pins and stick the shells neatly on to the paper with strong glue. Label each shell in white ink.

If you plan to take collecting really seriously get a copy of Puffin Picture Book No. PP120 called *Seashore Life*, which tells you about every kind of interesting thing to find when you're exploring the beach.

Stones on the Beach

Lots of beaches have beautiful stones if you will take the trouble to look for them, and some are even semi-precious. If you are old enough, borrow a book on stones from the library, it's worth learning how to recognize the different kinds.

Here are a few you may find: *cornelian*, *citrine*, *agate* and *onyx*. These are transparent when held up to the sun. They can be polished by a jeweller and made into jewellery. The cornelian is rusty-red. The citrine is pale yellow. Agate and onyx are banded, often with red, black and white lines. Agate has curved lines and onyx straight.

The way to find them is to walk along the shore towards the sun. When the pebbles are wet, you will easily see the transparent stones. You will also find glass fragments rubbed smooth by the sea, valueless but pretty.

Things to Do

A Bean Bag

A bean bag is easier to hold than a ball and, as it does not bounce, it is good for indoor play. To make it use old socks. Fill the toes about three quarters full with beans (or cherry stones, buttons, rags). Cut off the sock at the heel (Fig. 1). Turn the raw edges, and sew up the open end with strong thread. Decorate it, if you like, with material eyes, nose and mouth (Fig. 2).

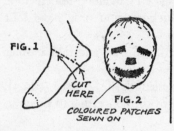

FIG. 1

CUT HERE   FIG. 2

COLOURED PATCHES SEWN ON

AUNT SALLY

Bean Bag Games

Aunt Sally

You need: a large piece of very stiff card, at least three feet long by two feet wide, paint, scissors or sharp knife.

1. On the card draw a head and cut round the outline.
2. On the head paint a face with a large, open, round mouth. Cut out the mouth leaving a hole.
3. Lean the Aunt Sally against a wall and stand four feet away. Throw the bean bag into Aunt Sally's open mouth.

A Team Game

Divide the players into two teams, giving each leader a bean bag. Teams stand in a line with their legs apart. The leader bending down throws the bag through the legs of the team to the last in the line. This player runs to the front and repeats the throwing. Continue until the leader is back at the start. The team whose leader gets back to the front first is the winner.

Paper Carnations

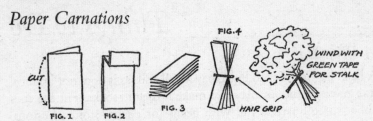

You need a face-tissue, hair grip, scissors.

These are realistic and easy to make:

1. Fold tissue in half lengthways (Fig. 1). Cut along folded edge. (As each tissue has a double thickness you now have four layers of tissue.)
2. Starting at one end fold half inch, turn over and fold another half inch (Fig. 2).
3. Repeat this 'concertina' the whole length of the tissue (Fig. 3).
4. Slide hair grip across the middle of the concertina to pinch it, but do not tear it (Fig. 4).
5. Holding the hair grip firmly in one hand, with the other start fluffing up each of the four layers of tissue. This makes the carnation.

Tissues can be bought in different colours so you can make a mixed bunch of carnations.

A Shell Box

Find a strong cardboard or tin box, or a match-box will do. Cover the underneath and sides with glue, and stick on pieces of velvet or ribbon, tucking the edges inside neatly. Leave to dry.

When quite dry, choose the shells you want to use on the top and decide exactly how you will arrange them. Lay them in order beside the box. Then melt sealing-wax (a pale colour is best) over the top of the box, a little at a time as it sets quickly, and at once, while it is still hot and soft, put the shells in place.

If the box is large enough you can even stick a postcard view of the place where the shells came from in the middle.

A Fish Mobile

You need one piece of card or 3-ply wood 9 in. by 8 in., two pieces of card or 3-ply wood 3 in. by 2 in., ruler, set-square, scissors or fret-saw, pencil, paint and brushes, black thread, pair of pliers, sealing wax, two feet (24 inches) of stiff florist's wire, balsa cement, drawing pins or paper clips.

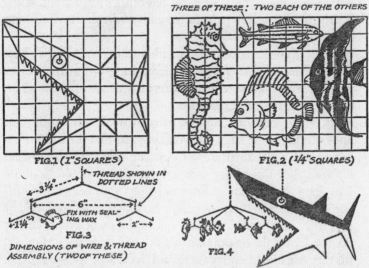

THREE OF THESE: TWO EACH OF THE OTHERS

FIG.1 (1" SQUARES)

FIG.2 (¼" SQUARES)

THREAD SHOWN IN DOTTED LINES

FIX WITH SEALING WAX

FIG.3
DIMENSIONS OF WIRE & THREAD ASSEMBLY (TWO OF THESE)

FIG.4

1. Along two adjacent edges of the largest piece of card or three ply, mark off one-inch intervals with your set-square, ruler and a sharp pencil. Complete the squares as in Fig. 1. Do the same on the two smaller pieces, this time using ¼-in. intervals.
2. Using the squares as a guide draw the outline of the shark on the largest piece (Fig. 1) and the four small fish on each of the other two (Fig. 2). Cut these out with a fret-saw or scissors.
3. Cut two pieces of wire 6½ in. long and sharply bend each of these in the middle until the ends are six inches apart. With the pliers turn the ends sharply up into tiny hooks of about 1/16 in. Bind the centres of the two wires together tightly with black thread (leaving about 4 in. of thread free) as in Fig. 3.
4. Cut four pieces of wire 2¾ in. long. Bend each sharply in the

centre until the ends are 2 in. apart. With the pliers turn the wire upwards at $\frac{1}{8}$ in. from each end, forming a right angle.

5. Paint the shark and fish on both sides (remember sharks are dark above and light below). When he is dry hang the shark up, using black thread attached by means of a drawing pin or paper clip to the edge just above his eye. Be sure he dangles within easy reach, clear of walls and other obstructions.

6. Fix the smaller fish in pairs to the ends of the short wires using blobs of hot sealing-wax.

7. Now attach 6-in. wire-cross assembly to the nose of the shark by the piece of thread you left free, using a drawing-pin or paper-clips for the time being. Leave a distance of about $2\frac{1}{2}$ in. between the nose and the wire.

8. Next, with great care, tie the pairs of small fish to the four hooked ends of the large cross making sure that the larger (sea-horses and angel fish) are on opposite sides and the smaller likewise. The threads by which the fish hang should be about $\frac{1}{2}$ in. long and the knots fixed as before with cement or nail-varnish. The mobile is now finished and the small fish should be able to swim cheerfully in and out of the shark's jaws. If they do not, loosen the thread at the shark's nose and raise or lower it till they are free, then fix the thread to the nose with a small pin pushed into the edge with the pliers, holding the pin firmly near the point, not the head. Trim off the extra thread. If the small fish still touch some part of the shark move the clip or pin holding up the shark slightly forward or backward till they are free. Hang the mobile where it will not obstruct the household traffic.

There is nearly always enough air movement to keep the mobile drifting. Now design your own mobile.

N.B. It is necessary to make *three* of the smallest fish (top of Fig. 2) to balance the pairs of the others, because they are much lighter. Mount two of these on the wire in the same way as the others and, after cutting a $\frac{1}{4}$-in. slot through the back fin of the third fish, cement this to the middle of the wire before attaching the thread.

Rag Doll

You need needles and cotton, wool, small buttons, scraps of material, cotton wool, flock or foam plastic for filling.

Head. Cut out a circle in material and turn in the edge with running stitch. Pull the thread to make a bag and stuff with filling. Pull together and finish off (Fig. 1).

Face. Embroider a face on the head (Fig. 2).

Body. Draw a body with legs and arms attached (Fig. 3). Pin on to the material and cut two the same. With the material turned inside out sew along one side with running stitch. Oversew on the right side, leaving the neck open.

Stuff legs and arms and finally the body. Sew up the neck.

Sew lines for fingers and toes (Fig. 4). For joints make a tiny row of running stitches (Fig. 5).

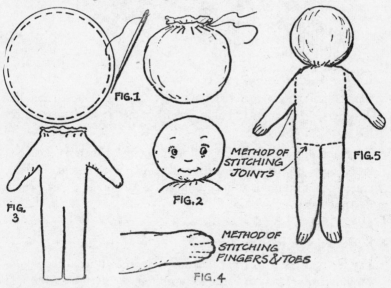

FIG.1

FIG.2

FIG.3

FIG.4

FIG.5

METHOD OF STITCHING JOINTS

METHOD OF STITCHING FINGERS & TOES

How to Cover a Doll's Head

You need 4-ply brown or yellow wool, a needle with a large eye.

1. Decide on the length you want the hair and cut sufficient

strands of wool to cover the back of the head from A to B (Fig. 1 overleaf). These strands will be folded in half so cut them double the length you need.

2. Stitch these in place from A to B, using a back stitch. When they are in place, sew back through each loop to secure them (Fig. 2).

3. Cut strands of wool to cover the head thickly from C to D. Using a back stitch, sew these in place down the centre of the head in bundles of four or five strands at a time (Fig. 3).

4. Trim the hair level all round, and either plait it or make a hairband from a small piece of ribbon and elastic.

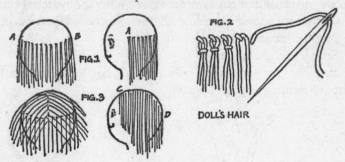

DOLL'S HAIR

Doll's Clothes and Accessories

Some hints: choose material that is soft, and fine. Thick material is difficult to sew, and too bulky. Keep stitches as small as possible, fasten off thoroughly.

To make doll's clothes you will need scraps of material, scissors, fastenings, press-studs, hooks and eyes, needle and bodkin, cottons, trimmings, lace and bindings, ribbon, braid, paper, pencil, narrow elastic.

Vest

Soft flannel or stretchy material.

Lay the undressed doll on paper and draw the outline of the doll's shoulders and from the arm to hips (Fig. 1). Remove doll and draw in waist and back of neck and armholes (Fig. 2). Draw this pattern twice, side by side (Fig. 3). Pin pattern on material and cut out. Tack together and fit. Hem round armhole and along waist edge. Join shoulder seams and side seams. Thread narrow ribbon round neck (Fig. 4).

A Vest from Old White Socks

Use previous pattern, but one half only. Lay the pattern on a piece of sock (double) preferably choosing a sock of the right

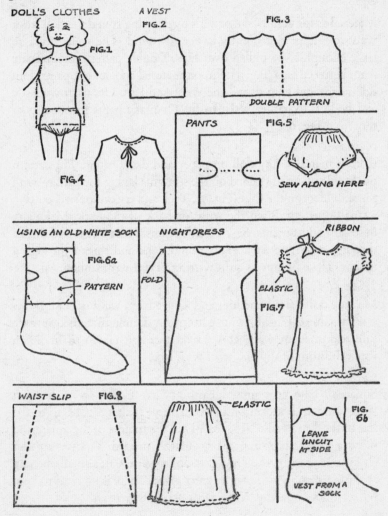

DOLL'S CLOTHES

FIG.1

A VEST
FIG.2

FIG.3

DOUBLE PATTERN

FIG.4

PANTS   FIG.5

SEW ALONG HERE

USING AN OLD WHITE SOCK

FIG.6a

PATTERN

NIGHTDRESS

FOLD

RIBBON

ELASTIC

FIG.7

WAIST SLIP   FIG.8

ELASTIC

FIG. 6b

LEAVE UNCUT AT SIDE

VEST FROM A SOCK

width so that no side seams are necessary (Fig. 6b). Cut along shoulder and waist and cut out armholes, keeping the neck opening wide enough for the doll's head. Immediately oversew raw edges or bind with bias binding to stop stitches running. Run narrow ribbon or draw thread round neck (Fig. 4).

Pants

Material as for vest. Make pattern by drawing round the doll from waist to thighs. Cut slightly larger all round. The waist must be large enough to be pulled over hips. Double pattern to eliminate seam between legs (Fig. 5). Pin on material and cut out pants. Join side seams and hem round the waist and legs. Use narrow elastic and bodkin to gather waist to fit. Or make pants from socks as shown in Fig. 6a.

Nightdress

Cotton material. Lay doll on paper and draw round. Pin pattern on double material (folded on the straight) laying the pattern with the shoulders on the fold (Fig. 7). Tack and try on for size, cutting a small opening down the front or back of the neck. Make any necessary adjustments. Sew up side seams. Hem wrists and thread through narrow elastic. Hem round neck and thread through a narrow piece of tape as a drawstring. Trim with ribbon.

Waist Slip

Measure doll's waist and hips and length from waist to hem. Draw a skirt pattern (Fig. 8). Cut pattern on double material. Sew up side seams. Hem waist and thread through elastic to fit. Hem round bottom of slip and trim with lace.

Circular Skirt

Square of felt; sides must measure twice the length of the skirt from waist to bottom, plus two or three inches according to the size of the doll's waist (Fig. 10a). Find the middle of the square and draw a circle according to the length needed. Draw a smaller circle in the centre, the size of the doll's waist. Cut a small opening at the waist and sew fasteners into place. There is no need to hem felt as it does not fray. Trim with braid (Fig. 10b).

Shoes

Scraps of felt left over from making circular skirt. Stand the doll on paper and draw round feet to make sole pattern (Fig. 11a). Draw a pattern for the front and side of shoes (Fig. 11b). Stick patterns together and fit on doll. Do this often until you have a good fit. Sew back of heel with coloured, stranded embroidery cotton. Sew top of shoe to sole. Trim with coloured felt (Fig. 11c).

Satchel or Handbag

Scraps of felt. Cut a piece of felt the size you want (Fig. 12). Fold and oversew side seams. Attach cord or ribbon according to the length required.

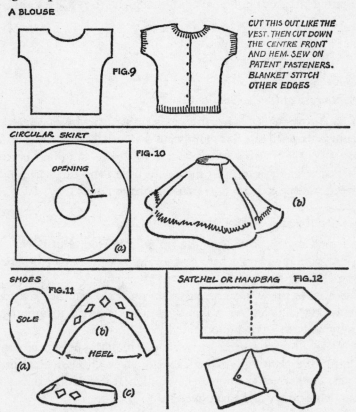

A BLOUSE

FIG. 9

CUT THIS OUT LIKE THE VEST. THEN CUT DOWN THE CENTRE FRONT AND HEM. SEW ON PATENT FASTENERS. BLANKET STITCH OTHER EDGES

CIRCULAR SKIRT   FIG. 10

OPENING

(a)

(b)

SHOES   FIG. 11

SOLE

(b)

HEEL

(a)

(c)

SATCHEL OR HANDBAG   FIG. 12

Indoors

Vegetable Tops

Use carrots, beetroots, turnips or parsnips. Cut off the tops leaving about ¼ in. only of the root. Trim the leaves back to about ½ in. of the root and put them root end downwards into a deep plate of water.

To make it look attractive, fill the bottom of the container with washed pebbles and wedge the vegetables between them. Keep the containers in a sunny place and top up with water. After a few days you will see the tops beginning to grow and they will continue to grow until quite tall, although no root will ever grow.

Out of Doors

A Marrow of One's Own

If you grow vegetable marrows in your garden, you can cut your name on a small one this month and then watch your name grow bigger as the marrow swells. Cut very gently and don't go too deep, just enough to open the skin a little. You can start a race with someone to see whose marrow grows fastest.

Holiday Garden

It is not always possible to dig up wild flowers. But if you do spend your holidays where it is allowed, you can try bringing home one or two plants to grow in your garden.

Sea pinks grow in sunny positions on stony soil. Sea lavender grows on cliffs and sand dunes. Heather is found in moorland country. In the woods, you could look for ferns.

You will need a small trowel and some little polythene bags. Dig up the plant with enough soil to cover all the delicate little roots. Put at once in a polythene bag. Don't shake more than you can help and try to replant quickly.

Games to Play

Oranges and Lemons

Choose two players to hold hands and form an arch, one to be Oranges, the other Lemons. The other children, forming a chain, march underneath singing the song:

'Oranges and lemons,' say the bells of St Clement's,
'You owe me five farthings,' say the bells of St Martin's,
'When will you pay me?' say the bells of Old Bailey,
'When I grow rich,' say the bells of Shoreditch,
'When will that be?' say the bells of Stepney,
'I'm sure I don't know,' says the great bell of Bow.
Here comes a candle to light you to bed,
Here comes a chopper to chop off your head.

At the words 'chop off your head' the 'arch' makes a chopping movement up and down and catches one of the children in the chain. The 'prisoner' is then asked to choose if he wants to be an orange or lemon. The other children must not hear his choice. He then joins on behind the leader of his chosen side. When all the children have been caught, the two teams have a tug-of-war.

Musical Bottles

You need seven empty bottles, a ruler, water.
Use any kind of bottles, provided they are all the same kind.
With seven bottles, you can tune them to a scale.

Fill the bottles with water, a different amount in each one.
Each level of water sounds a different note. Test the notes by tapping the bottle with a small piece of wood, such as a ruler. When you have tuned the bottles you will be able to play simple tunes on them.

Play this in the garden as you may spill some water.

August Cooking

Orange Cake

For the cake you need 2 6-in. sandwich tins, 4 oz. margarine, 4 oz. caster sugar, 2 eggs, 4 oz. self-raising flour, rind and juice of an orange. For the icing you need 4 oz. icing sugar, hot water, orange and lemon slices. Filling: lemon curd.

1. Grease and flour the sandwich tins.
2. Grate the rind and squeeze out the juice of an orange.
3. Beat the margarine and sugar together until they are soft and creamy.
4. Beat eggs and add gradually to the mixture, mixing all the time.
5. Blend in the flour.
6. Add the orange rind and juice.
7. Divide the mixture equally into the sandwich tins and smooth over evenly.
8. Bake in oven at 375°, regulo 6, for 20–25 minutes.
9. Cool on a wire rack and sandwich together with lemon curd.
10. Sieve the icing sugar into a bowl and add hot water, drop by drop, stirring all the time, till the mixture is pliable. Be careful not to get it too wet or the icing will run.
11. Dip a palette knife in hot water and spread the icing evenly over the sandwich cake and decorate with little orange and lemon slices which you can buy at the sweet shop.

September

Where the ripe pears droop heavily
The yellow wasp hums loud and long
His hot and drowsy autumn song:
A yellow flame he seems to be,
When darting suddenly from high
He lights where fallen peaches lie.

William Sharpe

Quarter Day

September is the end of summer and the beginning of autumn. Christina Rossetti wrote:

> The Spring is like a young maid
> That does not know her mind,
> The Summer is a tyrant
> Of most ungracious kind;
> The Autumn is an old friend
> That pleases all he can,
> And brings the bearded barley
> To glad the heart of man.

There are two Saints' days in September, St Matthew on the twenty-first and St Michael the Archangel on the twenty-ninth, so it is a special month for anyone called Matthew or Michael, and also for Marys, because 8 September is the birthday of the Virgin Mary.

Sometimes farmers who could not pay their rents on September quarter day gave their landlord a fat goose to soften his heart and an old rhyme says:

> Who so eats goose on Michaelmas Day
> Shall never lack money his debts to pay.

Queen Elizabeth is supposed to have been eating goose when, on 29 September 1588, she heard that her navy had defeated the Spanish Armada.

Starling

People sometimes mistake the starling for a blackbird, but the starling has a shorter tail and moves differently. The starling flies straight, often in large flocks, and on the ground *runs* busily about. Starling feathers are glossy and have a purple and green sheen. The starling is both a town and country bird. Thousands roost in city buildings, they twitter all the time as they roost, but their call is a grating *chirr*, sometimes developing into a musical whistle. They also imitate other birds. They make untidy nests of straw and feathers and lay from four to nine pale blue eggs between April and June. They stay in England all the year round.

Harebell

The harebell grows on rocky crags in dry, sunny places, as well as by the sea or on the moors. It is one of the commonest and most beautiful wild flowers. It has a slender stem, narrow leaves and pale-blue drooping bell-shaped flowers. When the harebell's stem is blown by the breeze its blue bells nod to and fro.

A Budgerigar

The budgerigar is an Australian bird. It is a pretty, friendly creature and not very expensive. It will cost from 10s. 6d. up to two guineas. A cage costs about 35s. 0d. It needs a water-pot and a pan of seed inside its cage, and either sand or special paper to keep the floor clean. Change and re-fill everything daily. If the seed-pot only needs topping up remove the old husks by gently blowing them off.

You can buy seeds in packets, or, a cheaper way, loose from a corn merchant. As a treat give the budgerigar some millet, but not too much or he will grow fat. He also likes to scrape his beak on a piece of chalky cuttle fish. Every day give him some fresh lettuce or other salad.

Budgerigars enjoy playing with toys and swings and admiring themselves in mirrors. They should have a bath at least twice a week and there are special baths made to fit on to the door opening of the cage.

If you want to teach a budgerigar to talk you must choose a very young bird, be very patient, and repeat each word, slowly, dozens of times every day. If you want to train it to sit on your finger you must be careful to move slowly or it will be frightened.

Put his cage in a sunny place but out of a draught, shade the cage in hot weather and, at night, cover it with a cloth.

Things to Do

Bowling Hoops

Hoops bowled with sticks are very ancient toys and are a traditional autumn game.

The bowler tries to make the hoop work very hard with as little effort from her as possible. If she is small and has a hoop as large as herself she can run in and out through the hoop as it rolls along (if she is clever and has set it on a straight course).

Two players, one with a small hoop, the other with a large hoop, can time the pace of their hoops so that they bowl the small hoop through the large hoop.

Turnpikes is a game for several players and one large hoop. The turnpikes (as many as there are players less the player with the hoop) are two stones set a little wider apart than the width of the hoop, and through these the hoop has to be bowled as fast as possible without touching. If it touches or misses, the turnpike holder takes the hoop and bowls until she misses.

Posting is a game for several players who stand at various points (in a circle is best, but a line will do) and one player with a hoop. This player starts the game and runs with the hoop, bowling as fast as she can, to the first post. He takes on the hoop, without stopping it for a second, to the next post, the arriving player filling the post of the leaving player.

When the game is played in a circle the hoop can be propelled round at tremendous speed.

Collecting Fungi (for older readers)

The lowest form of plant life (called Thallophyta) has two sorts of plants, fungi and algae. Algae are green and you see them growing in ponds. Fungi are different from algae because they have no green colouring matter (chlorophyll) and have to depend for food on organic (animal or plant) matter.

Fungi are either parasites, which means they live on living plants or animals, or saprophytes, when they live on dead plants or animals. Nearly all diseases of plants are caused by fungi (the others are caused by insects). Mildew on roses, blue mould on jam, witches' brooms on silver birch trees, and the green mould from which penicillin (a drug which can save the lives of people who are ill) is made, are all kinds of fungi.

There are many, many different kinds of fungi and they vary from a single, tiny cell which can only be seen through a microscope, to higher forms of fungi like the mushroom. Underneath, the mushroom is made of a mass of intertwined threads (hyphae) called spawn, above the spawn is a stalk formed of more tightly packed hyphae, on top of the stalk is a cap like an umbrella. Mushrooms, toadstools and puffballs are the most highly organized kinds of fungi. Lichens which you see growing on trees and rocks are a mixture of a fungus and an alga living together.

On an autumn walk it is interesting to see how many kinds of higher forms of fungi you can find. But they are very fragile and difficult to keep, so if you want to bring the most interesting ones home it is best to take a flat bottomed basket and a small trowel and handle them as little as possible. Take also a notebook and pencil. Write down where you find each one and make a note of the colours (as these soon fade), the texture and smell, and whether it was by itself or in a group. Then at home look them up in a reference book. This way you will soon learn to recognize the different types.

There are no rules for recognizing edible or poisonous fungi. Poisonous ones often peel as easily as edible ones. You will have to learn the characteristics of each one, particularly the very poisonous ones such as the Death Cap, which can be confused with the edible field mushroom and peels as easily. There are a number of edible fungi, among them large puff balls and blewits, but make quite certain that any you take home to be cooked are not poisonous ones.

Care of Your Sports Equipment

You need soap and water, dubbin, wax polish, linseed oil, blanco, cloths.

It is worth taking trouble to keep your sports equipment in good condition, as the better the equipment the better your game will be. When the season for any particular game is over, clean the tackle before putting it away.

Football, Netball and Rugger ball, Boots

1. Remove the mud and brush it out of the stitching.
2. Wipe the ball with soap and a damp cloth which has been soaked in warm water, then with a cloth wrung out in clean water.
3. Dry it and leave it overnight in the air.
4. Next day put on a small amount of polish or dubbin with a clean duster and rub it in. This will keep the leather supple.
5. In the spring, if you find the air has leaked out, take the ball to a sports shop and have it blown up and the lacing renewed if necessary.
6. Boots and shoes should be cleaned and polished in the same way. (The soft parts of the football and rugger boots should not be polished, but should have plenty of dubbin rubbed well in.) Check up on studs and replace damaged ones.

Hockey and Lacrosse

1. Wipe the mud off the sticks.
2. Rub the leather basket of the lacrosse stick with dubbin to keep it supple and clean, and the wooden stick with linseed oil.
3. If your rubber grip has torn or slipped down have it repaired or replace it.
4. If the varnish on your hockey stick is thin rub a little linseed oil or wax polish on it. This helps to keep the wood in condition.
5. Stand the sticks, handles downwards, in a corner or umbrella stand where they will not fall over.

Tennis

1. Wipe the edge of your tennis racket with a soft damp cloth, but be very careful not to dampen the strings.
2. If the varnish is damaged, rub over the outer rims with a very little linseed oil or wax polish.
3. Have any broken strings repaired.
4. Put the racket in a press. Be certain it is quite straight.
5. Collect tennis balls and put them in a plastic bag, beside your racket.

Cricket

Cricket bats are carefully made of good quality wood, but even the best will dry and crack if it is not properly cared for.

1. Wipe your bat with a damp cloth wrung out in a little warm soapy water.
2. Wipe dry with a cloth well wrung out in clean water.
3. When the bat is completely dry rub in plenty of linseed oil.
4. If the handle is not in good repair take it to a sports shop for a new rubber grip.
5. Rub the cricket ball with an oily cloth, to protect it where it is cut.
6. Pads should be cleaned with white blanco.
7. Cricket boots should be cleaned and studs examined and renewed if faulty.
8. Put all the equipment away together.

Swimming Equipment

1. After swimming, wash out your swimming suit in cold water.
2. Make sure also to wash flippers, goggles, snorkels and rings, removing all salt water and sand before you fold them up and put them away. (If you leave sand and salt water on them, they will rot.)

Things to Make and Do

Collecting Stamps

You need a small stamp album, stamp hinges, blotting paper, saucer of water.

As soon as you can read you can start to collect postage stamps. Begin by collecting stamps of all countries. A printed album with ruled spaces for the stamps is best for this. Try to keep them straight so that they look tidy. Torn stamps should not be used as they have no value. And you must be especially careful never to cut or damage the perforations round the edges.

Stamps should always be stuck into an album with stamp hinges. The hinge should be slightly damped at one end and stuck to the back of the stamp near the top. The remainder of the hinge should then be folded back behind the stamp, damped, and the stamp placed in position in the album. You should not use glue or stamp paper as these tend to discolour the stamps.

To start a collection, either buy a packet of mixed stamps or ask your family and friends to save stamps for you. Lots of people work in offices which have letters from abroad and, if you ask they may help you by keeping the envelopes. Keep duplicate stamps for swops.

Stamps stuck on to envelopes can be removed by floating the envelope, stamp upwards, in cold water for about 15–20 minutes, when the stamp will fall off easily and can be pressed and dried between clean sheets of blotting paper. *Any stamps dated before 1900 should be left on the envelopes, as these may be more valuable than the stamps.*

When you have enough, buy a loose-leaf album and use as many pages as you need for each country or group of stamps. A stamp catalogue is helpful in arranging stamps in the right order, date and value.

As stamp collecting is a hobby that 'comes and goes' it is wise to collect stamps from all countries, and never to throw any away. You may change your mind about which country interests you. For the same reason *never throw out your album*. Even if you stop collecting, one day it may be valuable.

Indian Head-dress

You need long feathers, corrugated cardboard, scissors, glue, adhesive tape, paint and brush, string.

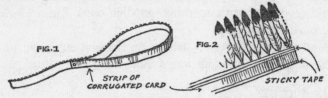

FIG·1 STRIP OF CORRUGATED CARD FIG.2 STICKY TAPE

1. With the scissors cut a length of corrugated cardboard about 4 ft long by 2 in. deep (Fig. 1).
2. Measure the size of your head with string just above the ears.
3. Place the string on the cardboard, marking with a pencil where to join it to make the head-dress.
4. If you wish, paint the feathers before you insert them.
5. Stick the feathers into the holes of the corrugated cardboard, working from the tail to the front, saving the largest for the front.
6. To hold the feathers in place, lay the head-dress on its side and stick adhesive tape along the bottom edge, and the back of the corrugated side (Fig. 2).
7. For a really dashing head-dress let the back hang down in a tail, also made with feathers.

Decorating Polythene Pots

You need empty cream or yogurt pots, scouring powder, poster paints, pencil.

These pots can be used for planting small autumn bulbs or decorating a dinner table with very tiny flowers, one in each place.

1. Clean the pot thoroughly inside and out, rubbing the outer surface gently with scouring powder on a damp cloth to remove the lettering.
2. With a pencil, design a pattern on the pot, as shown in the drawing, then paint the design using a fairly dry brush.

Wax Pictures

You need wax crayons, sheet of white paper, a blunt pencil.

1. Cover a table with thick newspaper to protect it, and lay a large sheet of paper flat on top.
2. Rub the crayon over the paper.
3. Draw a picture with a fingernail, or a stub of pencil. The lines you make will come out white on the colour.

Wax Faces

You need wax crayons, your hand.

1. Draw a face on the palm of your hand with crayon.
2. To change the expression on the face move your hand in different ways.

Parachute Man

You need a handkerchief, string, a wooden peg or soldier.

1. Take a square napkin, handkerchief or scarf, and tie a length of string about 12 in. long on to each corner.
2. Knot these at each corner of the handkerchief and leave four hanging cords.
3. Tie the four loose ends of string on to the soldier or peg man.

4. Roll up the parachute and throw it high in the air. It will open and the soldier or peg man will sail safely to land.

Orange Balls

You need an orange, ribbon, drawing pin, cloves.

1. Stick as many cloves as you can into a medium-sized orange.
2. Remove the calyx (the little knob on top of the orange), then put ribbon round it on four sides (in between the rows of cloves), tie on top with a bow and make a loop for hanging.
3. Put it into an airing cupboard to dry, and it will make a sweet-smelling present for Christmas. By hanging it in the wardrobe it will also help to keep the moths away.

Invisible Writing

You need a lemon or onion, small bowl, knife, pen, paper.

1. Squeeze the juice of the lemon or onion into a bowl.
2. Using the juice as 'ink', with a clean nib write a message on a piece of paper. Leave to dry. As it dries the message will disappear.

To make it reappear, hold the paper over a lamp or radiator. This is a very useful method of leaving extremely private messages, but you must be sure the person you are writing to knows how to 'develop' them.

Paper Butterflies

You need thin paper, a postcard, sheet of brown paper, pencil, crayons, glue, cotton, adhesive tape, hot oven or fire.

1. Draw some small butterflies on thin paper, colour, cut out.
2. Stick a piece of cotton 3 in. long to each one.
3. With adhesive tape fasten the end of cotton to the postcard.
4. Heat the sheet of brown paper in the oven for a few minutes.
5. Take it out and rub swiftly with even one-way strokes.
6. Quickly hold it over the butterflies on the card. They will fly.

As soon as the paper is cold they will drop, but to make them fly again reheat the paper.

Made with Cork

You need assorted corks, knife for cutting, used matches, pins. (Cork must be cut with a knife, so if you are not old enough to use a knife, ask an older person to help you.)

Dolls' House Furniture

The basic stool or table pattern: Cut a ring of cork about $\frac{1}{4}$ in. thick. Cut three or four matches in half for legs. Push the matches into the cork; pins may be used instead (Fig. 1).

To make a chair, insert four matches for legs and pin an extra ring of cork to the back. For an arm-chair add another ring of cork at either side. (Figs. 2 and 3).

For a standard lamp: a ring of cork $\frac{1}{4}$ in. thick for the base, and another ring about $\frac{1}{2}$ in. thick for the shade. Join the two rings of cork by a match (Fig. 4), or use a paper chocolate cup for a lampshade, or use a cotton reel for the base instead of cork (Fig. 5).

Animals are also easy to make (Figs. 6–8) and so is a boat (Fig. 9):

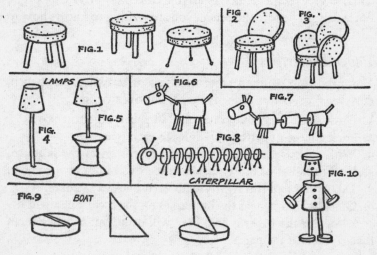

FIG. 1   FIG. 2   FIG. 3   LAMPS   FIG. 5   FIG. 4   FIG. 6   FIG. 7   FIG. 8   CATERPILLAR   FIG. 9   BOAT   FIG. 10

1. Cut a ring of cork about ¼ in. thick and make a shallow slit across it.
2. Cut a sail from stiff paper or cardboard and slip into slit (Fig. 9).

Fig. 10 is a man to look after the animals and sail the boat.

Musical Instruments

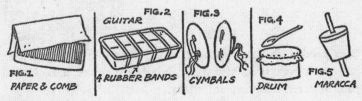

A Paper Comb

You need a comb, a sheet of tissue or toilet paper.

Fold the paper over the teeth of the comb (Fig. 1), put between your lips and blow and hum tunes.

A Guitar

You need a box lid, elastic bands.

Place the elastic bands across the box at regular intervals (Fig. 2).

Cymbals

Pass flat saucepan lids against each other and clash them (Fig. 3).

A Drum

You need a round box or tin, brown paper, a wooden spoon.

Tie a sheet of brown paper tightly over the open end of a round box or tin. Use a wooden spoon as a drum-stick, but be careful not to split the paper (Fig. 4).

A Rattle or Maracca

You need a carton with a screw-on top, a round stick about 12 in. long, a few grains of rice, glue.

Make a small hole at each end of the carton and put the stick through them. Put in a few grains of rice. Smear the screw edge with glue and screw on the top. Squeeze a little glue round the edges of both holes to keep the stick firm (Fig. 5).

Toffee Apples

You need 1 lb. brown sugar, 3 oz. butter, 1 dessertspoonful glucose, 1 breakfastcupful water, small firm apples, a thick saucepan, buttered dish or plate, sticks.

1. Wash and dry the apples; remove the stalks and fit wooden sticks in their place.
2. Heat the sugar and water slowly in a thick saucepan until the sugar has dissolved.
3. Add the butter and glucose and boil all together quickly until a little becomes hard and brittle when it is dropped in cold water.
4. Dip each apple quickly into the syrup, remove it and put on a buttered dish.

When all the apples have been dipped once, re-heat the toffee and dip each apple in again so that they have a good thick coating of toffee. Leave on the buttered dish until cold.

Toasted Cheese

You need bread, butter, cheese, salt and pepper.

1. Grate a small cupful of any firm cheese. Cheddar is one of the best for this recipe. If you like, add a little mustard, salt and pepper.
2. Toast a slice of bread, about $\frac{1}{4}$ in. thick, on both sides until it is light brown.
3. Butter the toast and cover with the grated cheese.
4. Put under the grill until the cheese begins to bubble and brown. Eat before it gets cold.

Indoors

Conkers and Acorns

Find some small flower pots with draining-holes at the bottom. Put in one or two stones for drainage, but do not block up the hole, then fill the pot with garden soil. For quick results soak the conkers and acorns overnight. Plant only one acorn or conker in each pot, an inch below the top. Keep in the dark and water regularly until a shoot appears, then bring it out into the light. Next spring the small trees will produce their first leaves.

It is very important to keep indoor plants damp. Tap the pots with your knuckles or a small wooden hammer, and if they sound hollow you must water them immediately.

Keep the soil loosened on the surface round the plant.

Out of Doors

Looking Ahead. Remember to collect flowers now to dry for Christmas bunches. Include barley and wheat from the edge of a field. Tie the stalks together and hang upside down in a warm dry place.

Michaelmas Daisy. These flowers bloom in September, and are often used to decorate churches for Harvest Festival. There are many varieties and some grow four to five feet high. The most common colour is lavender blue, but they also grow in shades of pink, blue and white. Plants may be grown from seed, or new ones made in spring by dividing old plants.

The garden needs to be tidied up this month, as some of the plants will begin to look straggly and die off. They will need to be cut back and thrown away.

Games to Play

Battleships

You need two players, four pieces of squared paper 12 squares by 12 squares, numbered A to L and 1 to 12.

Each player has one squared piece of paper, which represents the ocean, on which he marks his six ships, using five squares for a battleship, three squares each for two destroyers, one square each for two submarines, and one square for a corvette. You can put your fleet anywhere you like on the ocean, but remember not to let your opponent see where you have put them.

One player starts the game by firing his first 'shot', saying for example, 'I am aiming at A2, G9 and L10', naming three squares he thinks might be occupied by his opponent's fleet. Then he marks them down on his spare piece of paper so that he does not aim at those numbers again. The other player has to tell him whether he has made a 'hit' and crosses off the appropriate square or squares, though he need not tell his opponent which of his ships has been damaged. Then the other player fires his first 'gun' in a similar fashion, and so on. A ship is considered sunk when each square has been hit by the other player, and the winner is the first to sink his opponent's whole fleet.

Scavenger Hunt

Two or more players.

Ask your mother to give each player a list of objects to collect. There is a time limit, and the area to be covered must be clearly stated and will of course vary according to the ages of the players. A few items for the list are suggested here and could be varied according to the month and place:

Wild flowers, leaves, flint, feather, piece of string, acorn, used envelope.

This is a very good game to play at parties. Perhaps a small prize might be given for the player who finds the largest number of objects.

A Cardboard Code Game

You need white cardboard, two pins, pencil, ruler.
Sending messages in code is easy if you do it like this:

1. Cut two circles of cardboard 4 in. in diameter and two circles 3 in. in diameter. Lay each smaller circle on top of one of the larger ones and join by pinning in the centre.
2. Divide the circumference of all circles into twenty-six spaces and in each space put a letter of the alphabet.
3. Mark in the letters on the second code in exactly the same order and give it to your friend. The order of the letters on the two outer circles must be the same, and so must the order of the letters on the two inner circles.

To send a message state the key you have chosen, for example, L = B. This means that you place the circles so that the L on the outer circle is opposite the B on the inner circle.

By spelling out the real message on the inner circle you give the corresponding letters in the outer circle.

Your friend then works out the coded message and sends a reply.

Any number of codes can be worked out simply by moving round the outer and inner circles, but remember to state which key you have chosen.

Donkey

Three to thirteen players, a pack of old playing cards.

If three players are playing you need the following cards: four aces, four kings, four queens.

If four players are playing you need: four aces, four kings, four queens, four knaves.

If five players you need: four aces, four kings, four queens, four knaves, four tens.

Each player is dealt four cards, which are picked up and held in the hand. The object is to collect four cards of a kind, e.g. four kings, four tens, etc.

When the dealer says 'Go' each player takes one card from his hand, puts it face down on the table and slides it along to the player on his left, who looks at it to see if it is of any use to him. This continues while each player tries to collect his four of a kind. The moment a player has four of a kind, he quietly lays his cards on the table, and folds his arms. The other players must then quickly do the same, and the last player to lay down his hand is the loser. He then opens his 'score' with the letter D. The cards are shuffled, dealt again and another round is played in the same way. If the same player is the last to lay his hand down in this round he then adds the letter O becoming 'DO'. The game continues until one player has lost six times when his score would read 'DONKEY'.

Magic Cotton Reel

Make this, twist the match, put it down and watch!

MAGIC COTTON REEL

TACK

RUBBER BAND

THREAD THIS END OF RUBBER BAND THRO' BEAD & OVER MATCH

MATCH STICK

BEAD

October

I've brought you nuts and hops;
And when the leaf drops, why, the
walnut drops.
Crack your first nut and light your
first fire,
Roast your first chestnut crisp on the
bar;
Make the logs sparkle, stir the blaze
higher,
Logs are as cheery as sun or as star.

C. Rossetti

Hallowe'en

The 31 October is called Hallowe'en. It is the night when, according to folklore, witches, devils, fairies, hobgoblins and all the imps of earth and air hold their annual holiday. Years ago, people lit fires to keep these creatures away, but nowadays if we have fires it is for roasting chestnuts. However, we still dress up and have Hallowe'en parties; and people play the old game of ducking for apples floating in a bowl of water. These have to be caught between the player's teeth. The size of the apple you catch is supposed to show the size of your future fortune.

Once upon a time people used to change their jobs in October, and all towns and villages had fairs where one could see men and women who had left their old jobs, or young people who had never worked before, standing in the market place waiting for someone to offer them work.

The Jay

The jay is a brightly coloured bird with a pinkish-brown body, black and white crown feathers, which it raises to form a crest, and blue feathers barred with black and white on its wings. The most noticeable point about it in flight is the white rump which one sees as it flies away. As it is a very nervous bird, this is often the closest view one has of it. It is found widely in England and Wales, but only in a few areas in Scotland. It is usually seen in woods and copses but visits gardens in winter for food. It also has a most irritating habit of biting off the buds of flowers and shrubs. It has a very harsh loud call, and builds its nest rather low in the undergrowth, of twigs and a little earth. It lays five to seven eggs, olive or buff in colour.

October Flower

Autumn Crocus

One of the few flowers which blooms after its leaves have died. The leaves appear in March, feed the flower capsule, then wither during spring.

It is the same shape as the spring crocus, but a little larger.

It is the only truly British crocus. Spring crocuses come from middle and southern Europe.

A Hedgehog

Hedgehogs have a protective coat of sharp spines on the top and sides of their body, but the rest is covered only by coarse hair and is vulnerable to attack. A hedgehog has a very strong sense of smell and hearing and, as soon as he senses danger, he tucks away his head and legs and curls up the unprotected parts of his body so that his enemies find only a bundle of sharp spines sticking out in all directions. The hedgehog's worst enemies are the fox and the badger.

Hedgehogs usually waddle along slowly but they can run very fast on their short legs or roll downhill like a ball. They are good swimmers.

If you find one when it is very young it will grow quite tame. It is kindest to allow it to run about the garden and put food out each evening. Hedgehogs hunt all night and sleep during the day. If you prefer you can keep them in a shed or outdoor hutch. If possible make a separate sleeping compartment in the hutch. Fresh hay or dead leaves make the best bedding and should be changed often.

Feed him plenty of fresh water, bread and milk, eggs, raw or cooked meat, and any insects you can find. In his wild state he eats worms, slugs, beetles, mice and young birds.

Hedgehogs eat large meals during the summer to put on fat to keep them alive during their long winter sleep. They hibernate in November or December and make themselves a warm nest of leaves.

Hedgehogs don't live very long so, when you have kept one for a little time, it is nicest for him if you let him hurry off back to the woods again.

Out of Doors

Autumn Fruits and Berries

In autumn the leaves turn red and gold and yellow, and the hedges are hung with berries. This is the time when we see clusters of orange berries on the rowan or mountain ash, pink berries on the spindle tree, red crab-apples, nuts on the hazel and chestnut trees, and apples and pears in our gardens.

When you go for a walk, take a book with you to look up the names of the berries, or if you pick them, take them home in a box and look up their names before they shrivel. Never try eating them until you are certain what they are, as some are very poisonous.

Some edible berries need to be cooked before eating, for example, hips, the fruits of the wild rose which are made into rose-hip syrup, cannot be eaten raw because the bristly hairs inside them stick in your throat. Haws, the fruit of the hawthorn or may tree, are crimson and plentiful and are a favourite food of birds. Blackberries ripen from early September and are probably the most familiar fruit of all. Another black fruit, the sloe, is very bitter and leaves a dry taste in the mouth. The bullace looks like a damson but is pleasanter to eat.

If you look carefully you will see that the holly berries are turning red and those of the mistletoe beginning to ripen. The snowberry is another white one very noticeable in winter months when it is left on the bare twigs. Elderberries are made into wine, but too much of either the flowers or berries can be poisonous.

Some of the poisonous plants are the most brightly coloured. Both black and white bryony with their bronze leaves and red berries, which grow almost everywhere, are poisonous. The deadly nightshade is one of the most poisonous plants growing in this country. It belongs to the potato family and grows about three feet high, with large leaves and drooping flowers. The shiny black berries are about the size of small cherries. *Never touch one of these.* The woody nightshade is less poisonous and more common and is to be found in hedges, covered with bright green, red and orange berries. Another name for it is bitter sweet. The poisonous cuckoo pint, or wild arum, grows at the foot of hedges and in the autumn has a head of brilliant red berries. The roots of the cuckoo pint were once used to make starch for the ruffs people wore. The small black berries of the privet and ivy, and the deep pink ones of the yew, ripen in October, and none of these must be eaten.

Now is the time to look for the shiny brown conkers of

the horse chestnut (see p. 57). These are best just as they burst out of their cases. The sweet chestnut is good to eat and can be roasted or boiled when it is taken from its prickly case. Beech, cob and hazel nuts are also good to eat, but many of them are taken by the squirrels. Their cases can be made into animals and decorations.

Roller-Skating

Skates with wheels instead of blades were first used on the roads in Holland in 1770. A musical-instrument maker brought some to England and hoping to encourage people to buy them he wore them while playing his violin. As he played he skated amongst his audience, but when his music gathered speed so did his skates and, unable to stop, the poor man crashed into a mirror, upsetting both himself and the onlookers.

Later on, before there were indoor ice rinks, roller-skating used to be very popular. It still is with boys and girls. A pair of roller-skates is a good thing to ask for as a birthday present, provided you have a flat firm place on which to skate.

Looking After a Bicycle

1. With a bucket of water and a scrubbing brush, scrub off the mud and wash the bicycle wheels.
2. Wipe the bicycle with a cloth.
3. When dry, polish the saddle and painted parts with a clean soft cloth and some furniture polish.
4. Clean the wheel rims, handlebars and other chromium parts with soap and water and wipe with a dry cloth. It is a good idea to put some Vaseline (not too thickly) on the wheel hubs, rims and spokes and the handlebars, to preserve them from damp.
5. Always see that the tyres are pumped up to the correct firmness. You may damage the tyres and inner tubes if you ride with flat tyres, as the weight presses the steel frame into the rubber.
6. To clean the chain lay the bicycle on its side and rub the chain hard with a brush dipped in paraffin, turning the pedals at the same time.
7. Then, with an oil-can, oil it lightly along its length and the wheel-hubs. Wipe off the excess oil with a rag. The chain should look shining and work smoothly, but not drip. When not in use, a bicycle is best left upside down on newspaper, and covered with a polythene sheet.

Coal-hole-lid Rubbing

If you walk in city streets and look on the ground you may notice some attractive metal patterns. These are on lids of coal-holes, and are often rich in designs which can be used for embroidery.

You do this in the same way as brass rubbing and you will find the instructions on page 61.

October Indoors

Dressing Up in Hats and Masks

You need newspaper, thick paper, scissors, adhesive tape, glue, paints, sequins, needle and cotton, elastic.

A Crown

1. Cut a strip of stiff paper or cardboard 2 in. high and 2 ft long.
2. Spread this out flat, draw a zigzag edge, and cut it out.
3. Glue coloured paper and sequins on to this, and stick the ends together (Fig. 1).

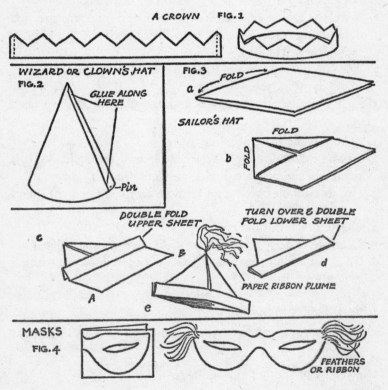

A CROWN   FIG. 1

WIZARD OR CLOWN'S HAT
FIG. 2
GLUE ALONG HERE
—Pin

FIG. 3
FOLD
a
SAILOR'S HAT
FOLD
FOLD
b

DOUBLE FOLD UPPER SHEET
c
A
B
e

TURN OVER & DOUBLE FOLD LOWER SHEET
d
PAPER RIBBON PLUME

MASKS
FIG. 4
FEATHERS OR RIBBON

A Wizard's Hat

1. Cut a sheet of thick paper so that it measures 12 in. by 18 in.
2. Put the paper flat on the table and paint magic signs on it, stars and lightning, dots and stripes, in purple and silver.
3. Fold into a cone shape and pin at the base.
4. Stick the edges firmly together with glue.
5. Remove the pin and cut round the large end to make it straight (Fig. 2, previous page).
6. Punch a small hole at each side and thread through some hat-elastic to hold it on the head.

A Sailor's Hat

1. Take a sheet of newspaper measuring roughly 12 in. by 18 in. Put this flat on the table and fold it in half (Fig. 3a).
2. With the folded edge farthest away from you, turn the two upper corners to the centre until they meet exactly and press them down (Fig. 3b).
3. Turn up the top layer of paper beneath the fold, on both sides of the hat (Fig. 3c).
4. Fold over corners A and B and fasten with adhesive tape.

Masks

1. Fold in half a piece of white paper.
2. Taking the folded edge as the centre, draw the outline of half the mask, and one eye (Fig. 4, previous page).
3. Cut this out and stick it on to some cardboard and cut round the outside edge.
4. Carefully cut out the eyes.
5. Decorate either by painting or sticking on coloured paper.
6. Trim by adding feathers (to the outside edge), or sticking sequins over it.

Pipe-Cleaner Models

Pipe-cleaners are wonderful for bending into all sorts of shapes.

A Giraffe (Fig. 1, opposite)
Use yellow or spotted pipe-cleaners.

1. Take two pipe-cleaners and bend the ends back to form the head and ears. Carry the long ends on down to form the neck, back and hind legs.
2. Take another pipe-cleaner and bend it to form the front legs. Make a figure of eight round the shoulders to strengthen them.
3. Wind a third pipe-cleaner round the ones already in place, starting from the nose, down the neck, and as far around the body as it will go.
4. Make a figure of eight round the hind legs with a fourth pipe-cleaner and wind it round the body, leaving an end to make a short tail.

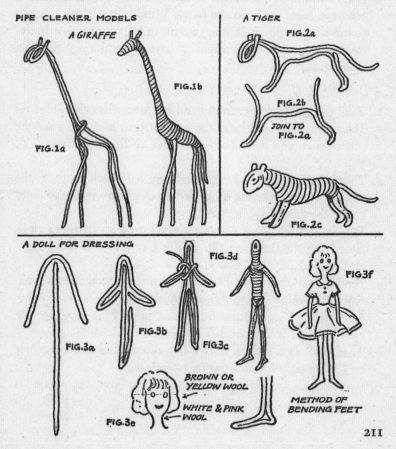

PIPE CLEANER MODELS

A GIRAFFE

FIG.1b

FIG.1a

A TIGER

FIG.2a

FIG.2b

JOIN TO FIG.2a

FIG.2c

A DOLL FOR DRESSING

FIG.3d

FIG.3f

FIG.3a

FIG.3b

FIG.3c

BROWN OR YELLOW WOOL

WHITE & PINK WOOL

FIG.3e

METHOD OF BENDING FEET

A Tiger (Fig. 2)

Use orange and black or yellow and black speckled pipe-cleaners if possible.

1. Take two pipe-cleaners and bend them back to form the head and ears. Bend one long end down to make the right front leg as shown, bending it up again to join the other one. Take them both on to form the body and back legs.
2. Make the back right foot with another pipe-cleaner, bringing it up along the body and down to form the left front leg (Fig. 2b).
3. Join in another pipe-cleaner at the nose and wind it round the others to form the head and body. Wind it in a figure of eight round the shoulders. Join in one more to complete the body, making a figure of eight round the back legs finishing off with a tail (Fig. 2c).

A Doll Which Can Be Dressed (Fig. 3. previous page)

1. Take two pipe-cleaners and bend one over the other (Fig. 3a) Take one down and bend the end to form one leg. Take the other down and bend both ends back to form the arms (Fig. 3b).
2. Take another pipe-cleaner, bend one half back to form the second leg and take the other half up to make a figure of eight round the shoulders (Fig. 3c).
3. Wind another tightly round the head, make a figure of eight round the shoulders on top of the first one and wind it on around the body (Fig. 3d).
4. Bind firmly round the body with some pink, white or fawn wool, finishing off any loose ends with a needle.
5. Sew eyes and mouth on to the face, using blue wool for the eyes and red for the mouth (Fig. 3e).
6. Thread the needle with brown or yellow wool and make hair by sewing tight loops all over the head.
7. Finally dress the doll with clothes made from any scraps of material you have (Fig. 3f).

Conker Tables and Chairs

You need conkers, pins, scraps of coloured wool, scissors.
Collect some conkers of various sizes. Polish them until they shine.

A Conker Table

1. Take four pins and the largest conker you have.
2. Turn the conker so that the pale circle is towards you.
3. Carefully push in the four pins in the form of a square; do not push them in too far, only until they are firm.
4. Stand the table on its legs, and, if necessary, adjust the pins so that the table does not wobble (Fig. 1).

Chairs

Use smaller conkers. Do the legs in the same way as for the table. To make a back for the chair put two pins in the top of the conker, just above one pair of legs, and wind a length of wool alternately round the pins. Fasten off by passing the pin head through the strand and cutting off neatly (Fig. 2).

For armchairs use four pins for the sides and back and weave wool round the three sides (Fig. 3).

Make stools (Fig. 4) with small conkers and only three legs.

Autumn Leaves

Leaf Prints

You need a soft crayon, a sheet of white paper.

1. Lay a leaf on a newspaper or a sheet of thick cardboard with the veins on the back of the leaf facing upwards.
2. Place a sheet of clean white paper over it, hold firmly in place.
3. With a very soft crayon rub lightly backwards and forwards across the paper until the leaf is completely covered. This will give a print of the pattern of veins on the leaf.

Spatter Prints

You need an old toothbrush, a knife, a sheet of paper, pins, poster paint or Indian ink.

1. Place the leaf on a sheet of white paper and pin it carefully in place.
2. Dip a toothbrush into poster paint or Indian ink thinned with water.
3. Hold the brush over the paper and scrape the bristles towards you with a knife. The ink will spatter on to the paper, outlining the leaves with a pattern of tiny dots.
4. Leave until quite dry, then remove the leaf.

Carbon Prints

You need a sheet of white paper, a sheet of carbon paper.
This can be done with leaves at any time of the year. Pick the leaf and press it between newspapers or blotting paper for twenty-four hours to absorb any moisture.

1. Place the leaf face down on a newspaper.
2. Place the carbon paper face down over the leaf and another newspaper over this.
3. Rub gently over the leaf with your thumbnail, making quite sure to cover it all.
4. Remove the newspapers and carbon paper and place the leaf, face upwards, on the white paper so that the carbon-coated veins are resting on the paper. Be very careful not to move the leaf or the print will be spoiled. Cover it with a piece of newspaper and smooth gently over it with your thumbnail once more. Remove the newspaper and leaf carefully and the carbon print will be left on the paper.

Preserving Leaves

You need autumn leaves, paraffin wax.

1. Melt a lump of paraffin wax slowly in a saucepan.
2. When it is quite soft hold a leaf by its stalk and dip it into the wax until it is completely covered.

3. Shake off any surplus drops and put the leaf down carefully on waxed paper or a wire tray. The wax can be used for many leaves.

Paper Trees

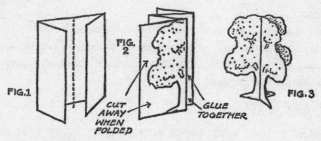

You need stiff paper or thin card, pencil, scissors, paints, glue. These trees can be made any size you wish.

1. Take a piece of paper twice the width and size you want the finished tree to be and fold it in half creasing it down the centre. Then open it out and fold in both sides to the centre crease (Fig. 1).
2. Fold the paper as in Fig. 2 and draw half a tree on the top fold. Cut round the tree, then glue centre faces together. This makes a three-sided tree (Fig. 3). Paint it either green for summer or yellow-brown for autumn.

Turnip Lanterns (for Hallowe'en Parties)

You need a large turnip or swede, knife and spoon, wire, skewer, candle.

It is fun to make these for Hallowe'en and keep them to carry to your bonfire on Guy Fawkes' Night.

1. Slice off the turnip about 2 in. from the top to form a lid.
2. Scoop out the inside of the turnip with a knife, leaving about 1 in. of 'shell'.
3. Cut out two eyes, a nose and a mouth – the easiest kind are shaped like triangles.

4. Pierce two small holes with a skewer near the top of the turnip.
5. Thread a piece of fairly stiff wire through these, long enough to make a comfortable handle to hold.
6. Scoop a little hole inside the turnip at the bottom for the candle to fit into, and twist the wire round it to make it secure.
7. Pierce a few holes in the lid to act as chimneys for the smoke from the candle and put it back on the turnip. When the candle is lit, light will shine brightly through the eyes, nose and mouth of the lantern.

Hallowe'en Man

You need 1 apple, white paper, scissors, glue, matchstick, cloves or pins, saucer.
If you are having a Hallowe'en party, here is a simple decoration you can make for the table.
1. Draw a circle round a saucer on the white paper. Cut out the circle. Cut a slit from the edge of the circle to the centre.
2. Fold to form a conical hat. When it is the right size for the apple, glue the edges together and stick on.
3. Put some glue on the lower half of the apple and stick on some cotton wool to form a beard.
4. Use half a matchstick for a nose and cloves or small coloured paper circles for eyes.

Modelling with Papier-mâché

You need an old newspaper, 2 large bowls, cupful of wall-paper paste, water.
Do this where it doesn't matter if you make a mess, and wear old clothes, or an apron.
1. Tear the newspaper into small pieces.
2. Put the pieces into a bowl and pour water over them. Make them very wet, then squeeze them as dry as possible.
3. Put the pieces into another bowl and sprinkle over them a cupful of wall-paper paste.

4. Mix the paper and paste with your fingers so that each piece of paper has paste on it.
5. Add water a little at a time and go on squeezing until the paper is mushy and feels sticky. If it does not feel sticky add more paste.
6. At this stage the paper can be moulded into any shape, heads of puppets or dolls, or flat surfaces for trays. If making a bowl, do not forget to make a flat base so that it does not wobble!
7. Put the shape in a warm, dry place to dry slowly. After a week it should be dry and can be painted and varnished.

An Oven or Coal Glove

You need needlecord, flannel or other lining, felt, needle, thread, scissors, bias binding or ribbon, glue.

You can use this as a coal glove, or an oven glove to help you carry hot things. Use dark colours for the coal glove and bright colours for the oven glove.

1. Lay your hand, or an adult's hand, flat on a sheet of paper (Fig. 1, overleaf), and draw round it, leaving a wide margin. It should measure at least 5½ in. across the wrist and 9½ in. from wrist to fingertips.
2. Lay the material for the back of the glove on the table. Pin the pattern on it and cut out. If you are making two, remember to turn the pattern for the second glove.
3. Lay out the material for the palm. This is usually the same both sides, but if you do cut out a pair remember to turn the pattern in case it should vary.
4. Cut another palm from the lining (Fig. 2). Place the back and palm on top of each other, right sides together, and the lining on top of the palm (Fig. 3).
5. Stitch the three layers together, leaving a ½-in. seam and using back stitch. You may need to make a small slit in the material by the thumb to prevent puckering (Fig. 3.) Don't cut through the stitches.

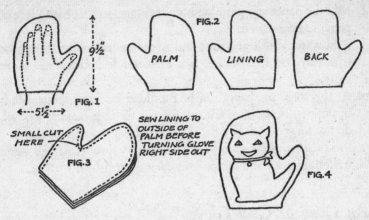

6. Turn the glove back to the right side and either turn the ends in at the wrist and hem them, or bind them with bias binding or coloured ribbon.

To decorate the glove with a cat, cut pieces of black or coloured felt for the head, body, legs and tail. Stick these on with a strong glue. When dry, embroider eyes, nose, mouth, whiskers and claws in contrasting colour.

Autumn Pictures

You need blotting-paper or newspaper, a heavy weight, thick paper, stiff cardboard or wood and some glass the same size, scissors, passe-partout, glue.

Autumn leaves are beautiful colours and shapes. Collect some perfect ones; also some grasses, to make a pattern.

Press the leaves and grasses between two layers of blotting-paper to absorb any moisture. Put under a flat heavy weight. Leave for several days. When dry, arrange them on a piece of thick white or coloured paper (absorbent paper is better than shiny). Coloured paper alters the tone of the leaves. Dab a little glue under each. Back the paper with wood or cardboard and cover it with the glass. Bind the edges tightly with passe-partout.

Indoors

Bulbs

Indoor bulbs grow best in fibre, because it holds moisture better than soil. Hyacinths planted now flower at Christmas. Daffodils, tulips, and mauve crocus can also be grown. (Yellow crocus do not flower indoors.) Soak fibre in water and squeeze. Put some in the bottom of a bowl and arrange the bulbs fairly closely. Cover with more fibre, leaving the tops just showing. Keep them moist and in the dark. As soon as they start to grow, bring the bowl to the light. Keep moist.

In water. There are special glasses which are filled almost to the neck with rain water, to which some charcoal has been added. The bulb goes on top and the roots grow down into the water. Do not wet the bulb.

Another method is to fill the bottom of a small tray with clean pebbles and rain water and wedge in bulbs. Do not wet the bulbs, but keep topped up. Bulbs grown in water need not be kept in the dark.

Outdoors

As the frost comes, dahlias, asters, petunias and salvias look sad; their heads drop and their leaves turn black. Dig them up. Dry and store the dahlia tubers away from the frost.

Plant daffodil, tulip, crocus and grape hyacinth bulbs for the spring now, also wallflowers, polyanthus and forget-me-nots.

Fortunately, some flowers are not hurt by the first frosts, and Michaelmas daisies, roses and chrysanthemums often go on flowering until November.

Games to Play

Conkers

A game for two players. You need conkers, string.

Make a hole with a skewer through two conkers and bake them in a slow oven for a few hours to harden them. Then thread a piece of string, about 12 in. long, with a large knot at one end, through each conker.

To Play the Game

One player holds out his conker on its string and steadies it, while the other player wraps the string of his conker round the four fingers of his right hand, leaving about 4 in. to pull back against his thumb. Then, holding the conker in his left hand, and pulling it firmly against the thumb of his right hand, he lets it go with a jerk and tries to hit the conker held still by the other player.

If he scores a direct hit and shatters the other player's conker, his conker becomes a 'oner'. The next time he scores a hit, it becomes a 'twoer' and so on. If the conker he shatters is already a 'twoer' he adds two on to his score, plus one for breaking the conker.

When playing this game do be careful to hold the conker well away from your eyes as, if it shatters, bits fly about.

Heads and Bodies

You need paper approximately 2 in. by 8 in. for each player, a supply of pencils, and any number of players.

1. Each player draws a head on the top of his paper with a neck below and folds his paper over so that only a little of the neck is showing. At the command 'Pass' he passes his paper to the player on his left, receiving in exchange one from the player on his right.
2. Each player draws a body on to the neck, finishing at the top of the legs. This he folds again, leaving a little of the legs showing and exchanging papers as before.
3. Each player adds legs and feet and folds the paper, leaving only a blank space showing and passes again.
4. Finally each player adds a name and folds the paper once more. The papers are then jumbled up, each player chooses and unfolds one of them, and they all look at the results together.

Pelmanism

You need a pack of playing cards, or a special pack of cards with pictures on them. Any number of players.

This is a good game to train memory and observation. The aim of the game is to collect as many pairs as possible. The cards are laid face down on the table. The player on the left of the dealer starts by turning two cards over, showing the other players what they are. If they are a pair, such as two 3s or 8s or kings, he picks them up, but if they are two different cards he must lay them face down again in exactly the same place. The other players must note the cards and try to remember them. The next player on the left then turns up two cards. If one of these is the same as a card turned up by the first player, he may take the pair, provided he can remember where the original card was, and then have another turn. If he turns up a different card by mistake, he must replace it. The game continues until all the cards are matched, the winner being the one with the most pairs.

If you have not played this game before, try using only twelve or eighteen cards at first, making sure you choose six or nine pairs, until you become used to remembering them. As you improve, add more cards.

October Cooking

Baked Apples

For two people you need 2 large cooking apples, syrup or brown sugar, sultanas or currants.

1. Wash and carefully take out the core of each apple.
2. Place apples on a buttered baking tin, and into the holes left by the removal of the cores place a dessertspoonful of syrup or brown sugar and a few sultanas or currants.
3. Bake for 30 minutes at 300°, regulo 3.

Serve with whipped cream or custard.

November

I love to see the cottage smoke
Curl upward through the trees,
The pigeons nestling round the cote
On November days like these;
The cock upon the dunghill crowing,
The mill sails on the heath a-going.

John Clare

Guy Fawkes

The Romans, for whom November was the ninth month (its name comes from the Latin word *novem*, nine), considered 11 November the beginning of winter. Although real winter for us usually doesn't begin until after Christmas.

'Remember, remember the fifth of November.' Everyone knows about Guy Fawkes. He was a Yorkshireman who joined in a plot to blow up the Houses of Parliament. He hid thirty-six barrels of gunpowder in a cellar under the House of Lords, and what a bang that would have made, if the plot hadn't been discovered. Guy Fawkes was arrested and executed and although he showed great courage we have been making models of him and burning him on bonfires ever since.

Every year, on the second Saturday in November, the colourful pageant of the Lord Mayor's Show can be seen in London.

The Chaffinch

Finches are a large bird family of about 200 species. They include some of the commonest British birds such as chaffinches. They all behave in much the same way, but their plumage differs greatly. The chaffinch is a typical finch. In summer they go about in pairs, but generally in winter they fly about in flocks of separate sexes. They make beautifully built little nests of moss and wool, lined with hair, and their eggs are a pale purplish-grey spotted and streaked with red. They generally build their nests in shrubs, hedges or the low branches of trees. Their song is not very attractive and varies according to the time of year.

The male has a slate-blue crown, a chestnut mantle, a throat and breast of burnt sienna. The female is duller with an olive-green back. Both sexes have an easily seen white patch on the shoulders.

Firethorn

There are not many wild flowers to be found this month, but you may find deadnettle, yarrow and shepherd's purse, and many walls and fences have pyracantha growing against them. It is evergreen and has bunches of scarlet berries. It is also called firethorn.

A Dog

A dog is the most faithful pet you can have. If you have a chance to choose one, whether pedigree or mongrel, pick one the right size for your house and garden. It is not fair to keep a very big dog in a small house.

Most dogs need two meals of meat and biscuits a day, and a bowl of fresh clean water always available. A puppy will need smaller and more frequent meals. As each breed requires a different amount, ask your vet's advice.

As soon as possible after he is six weeks old a puppy should be inoculated against distemper and hardpad. Do not let him out of the garden until this has been done. To housetrain him, take him out regularly to the same place, and he will soon learn.

He will need a collar and lead, but do not spend too much money on them, as they may be chewed. You should be able to put two fingers between his neck and the collar; remember that his neck will grow! All dogs should be brushed and combed each day.

A reward for doing the right thing helps a dog to learn obedience. Always use the same words of command, and keep them simple. If you have dog-training classes near you, it would be helpful to attend them.

When a dog is six months old he needs a yearly licence. This costs 7s. 6d. at the Post Office.

A Dog Bed

A dog needs a strong, draught-proof bed. Here is one to make (Fig. 1). For a spaniel or other medium-sized dog, the bed should be about 21 in. long and 16 in. wide (internal measurements). A larger dog will need it 3–4 in. longer and 2 in. wider.

You need 4 ft 6½ in. of boarding 6 in. wide for the sides and back, 7½ ft of boarding 3 in. wide by ¾ in. thick for the front and floor support, plywood or hardboard 16 in. by 21 in., saw (tenon saw if possible), set square, hammer, 30 nails (2 in. long), one sheet of medium sandpaper, ruler or tape measure.

From the 6 in. board cut one piece 22½ in. long for the back and two pieces 16 in. long for the sides. Shape corners (Fig. 2). Cut the 3 in. board into four 22½ in. lengths for the front and floor supports. Nail the back and front to the sides (Fig. 3) making sure the frame is square. Turn the box over and nail on the floor supports (Fig. 4). Cut the plywood to fit inside the frame. Hammer all the nails well in, and finish by sandpapering all corners and rough edges, especially the back.

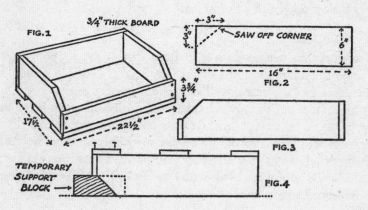

FIG. 1 3/4" THICK BOARD

SAW OFF CORNER

3"
3"
16"
6"

FIG. 2

3¾"

17½"   22½"

FIG. 3

TEMPORARY
SUPPORT
BLOCK

FIG. 4

Out of Doors

A Guy

You need a sack, straw and/or newspaper, string, needle and cotton, 4 old stockings, small bag, piece of light-coloured material 1 ft square, buttons for eyes, old clothes.

The sack is for the body. Stuff this as full as you can with straw or newspaper made into tight balls, until it is firm. It is a good idea to put a long stick into the sack before you close it to keep it rigid. Stuff four stockings, and a small bag for the head, in the same way. Sew the head, arms and legs on to the body, or tie them on with string.

Paint a face on some material and attach to the guy, then dress it with old clothes and a funny hat.

Fireworks

Fireworks contain explosives and are dangerous, so you must handle them very carefully. Before Guy Fawkes' Night they should be stored in a dry place, well away from any fire or matches. On 5 November put all fireworks in a thick cardboard or tin box and keep the lid on, except when you are taking any out, so that they are not set off by mistake by a stray spark. Set up these holders beforehand so that you can let off your fireworks easily and safely:

A Flat Board or piece of wood to let off aeroplanes, flying saucers, bangers, etc.

A Large Bottle to stand smaller rockets in, and a post with two staples driven into it 12 in. apart to set off larger rockets.

A Seed Box filled with soft ashes or sand to take Roman candles and other fireworks of that type.

Always read the instructions on the fireworks carefully and obey them word for word. Never carry fireworks in your pockets and never, never throw them at other people.

Hopscotch

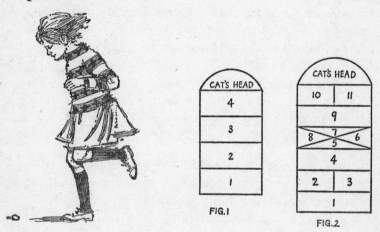

FIG. 1

FIG. 2

You need a piece of chalk to mark out the game, a shell or flat stone for a pitcher.

Hopscotch is an ancient game and many variations of it are played in different parts of the country. In its simplest form the game is played in rectangular courts drawn on the ground (Fig. 1). The player begins by throwing the pitcher into the first court and then hopping over the line and knocking it back with the point of his toe. He repeats this in courts 2, 3 and 4, and finally in the Cat's Head, each time kicking the pitcher back into court 1 before throwing again.

In a more complicated game the court is divided and marked with numbers 1–11, until the top space, number 12, which is called Cat's Head or Plum Pudding (Fig. 2). On the halved courts, the player must stand astride, on the plain courts, on one foot. On the fourth and ninth courts he stands on one foot and jerks up the pitcher and catches it. On the final journey to the Cat's Head he must advance like this:

Hop on 1, stand astride in 2 and 3, hop on 4. Stand astride in 5, 7, 6 and 8, hop on 9. Stand astride in 10 and 11 and hop on the Cat's Head. On the Cat's Head the player must lift the pitcher by jerking it up with his toe, catch it and replace it on the ground. He must do this three times in succession without dropping his other foot. At the third time, with one kick, he must drive the pitcher through all the courts to the start, and return down the courts the way he came.

Rules for Both Games

A player is out if he throws on the wrong court, throws on the lines, hops off the court, changes feet, or steps on a line.

Collecting Feathers

You need a drawing book, adhesive tape, scissors.

Bird's feathers are fun to collect and can teach one a lot about different birds and how to identify them.

You can collect feathers from birds which have been shot in the autumn and winter months, such as pigeons, partridges, pheasants and ducks, and whose feathers can be picked up in the fields; or ask your butcher to keep you the feathers from the birds he plucks.

Birds moult in the spring and summer, and if you look on the ground, especially near pools of water where they bath and under trees where they nest, you can often find dropped feathers.

Mount the feathers in a drawing book. Arrange them nicely and stick a small piece of adhesive tape over the quills to secure the feathers. Write the name of the bird from which it came under each one, the date, and the place where it was found.

You will be surprised how many kinds of feathers you will find. Try to find out also what part of the bird the feathers came from. You will easily know the soft down from the breast, but it will be harder to tell the feathers from the different parts of the wing.

Twig and Branch Shelter

You need three strong branches 4 ft–5 ft long (if possible one of them with a fork at one end), string, twigs, smaller branches.

Place the branches against each other, resting the ends of two of them on the forked branch. Bind them together firmly with strong string. Leave one side open for the entrance, facing away from the direction of the wind, and pile small branches and twigs against the other two sides. Press them down very firmly to make the walls as thick as possible.

Feeding the Swans

Swans and ducks living on ponds and lakes have lots of visitors in the summer bringing them scraps, but in the hungry winter weather they have fewer visitors and fewer tit-bits. So, if you know some swans or ducks near where you live don't forget them in the winter. Go and see them and take with you a fat bag of bread bits. They'll be very pleased, although you may find that some of the swans have gone to the sea till spring.

Things to Make and Do

Ghost Dancer

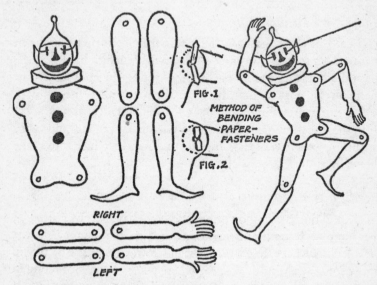

FIG. 1

METHOD OF
BENDING
PAPER-
FASTENERS

FIG. 2

RIGHT

LEFT

You need a large piece of cardboard, 8 brass split-pin paper-fasteners, scissors, knitting-needle, cotton.

1. Copy these drawings of the body on to the cardboard.
2. Cut out the nine parts of the body and paint in any colours you choose.
3. Make a hole with a knitting needle through all the points marked.
4. Join the right upper arm to the body with a paper-fastener by pushing the paper-fastener through the hole at the top of the upper arm and through the hole in the shoulder (Fig. 1). When it is through, open the fastener and bend the points over (Fig. 2).
5. Attach the right lower arm to the upper arm in the same way. Do the same with the left arm and both legs, making sure you

have them in the correct position, or the feet will point inwards.

To make the ghost dance, take about 8 ft of black cotton and tie one end to the leg of a chair, about 12 in. from the floor, pass the end behind the other leg of the chair and tie a loop in the end of it.

Carefully pull the cotton into small cuts at the top of the ears, so that it passes behind the head and comes out through each cut. Then as the cotton is gently pulled taut the ghost will stand up; if the cotton is jerked he will jump and wave his arms and legs. If the chair is put against a dark background, the cotton will not show and if the hand moving it is kept out of sight, no one will know how it is made to dance.

Alphabet Doodling

Draw some letters and then see how many different things you can turn them into. Here are some we have done.

Clay Modelling

You need modelling clay (not plasticine), a wooden spatula (or a teaspoon with no decoration on the handle), a wooden skewer, a blunt knife, a board or tray to work on.

It is extremely important to keep the clay soft enough to be workable. To achieve this you must wrap the clay in a damp cloth

233

and keep it in a tin with an airtight lid or in a plastic bag whenever you are not using it, or it will become too hard to use.

When you start modelling, wear an overall, and work on a tray or board on a table. Put a lump of clay on the board and try squeezing it, then pull it about and break off pieces, and stick them on again. Roll it, make sausages of it, cut it, squash it into different shapes, until you get the feel of it.

You will find you can make animals, people, anything, in fact, that you wish. You should build up animals (or whatever you decide to make) by adding pieces on to one another. In this way, what you make grows out of handling and adding.

When you have finished your model, leave it safely to dry for a few days. When it is thoroughly dry you can give it a coat of shellac (which can be bought from a builder's merchant) using a soft brush. This will seal it so no air or moisture gets in. You can then paint it with either oil paint or enamel colours.

How to Make Pots

Thumb Pot

1. Take a lump of clay which is big enough to hold comfortably in one hand, and roll this into a smooth ball.
2. Make a hole in this by sticking your thumb in the centre of the ball (not out through the bottom though).
3. Keeping your thumb on the inside, slide the clay round in your hand while you squeeze it between your fingers and the thumb.
4. Continue to turn and squeeze, but widen the rim at the upper edge, and gradually, with the same movement, mould your pot until it is of even thickness and is circular throughout.
5. Leave to dry.
6. Coat with shellac.
7. Paint it.

Coil Pot

1. Roll out an even worm of clay about as thick as a pencil and as long as you can make it.

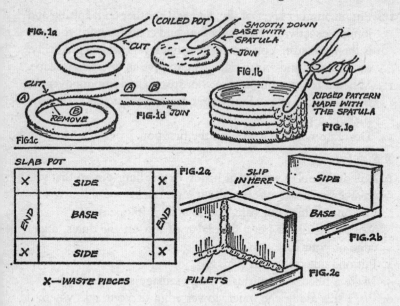

FIG.1a (COILED POT) SMOOTH DOWN BASE WITH SPATULA
CUT
JOIN
FIG.1b
CUT
A
A B
REMOVE
FIG.1d JOIN
FIG.1c
RIDGED PATTERN MADE WITH THE SPATULA
FIG.1e

SLAB POT
FIG.2a
SLIP IN HERE
SIDE

X	SIDE	X
END	BASE	END
X	SIDE	X

SIDE
BASE
FIG.2b
FILLETS
FIG.2c
X—WASTE PIECES

2. Coil this round in a spiral until the base of your pot is the size you want it to be (Fig. 1a).

3. Take your knife and cut off the end, and join it on smoothly.

4. Take your spoon handle, or wooden spatula, and gently smooth over the ridges on the upper side of the work (Fig. 1b).

5. Make yourself some 'slip' by taking a walnut-size piece of clay and mixing it in a cup with a few drops of water, until it is of the same consistency as cream.

6. With a finger put a thin layer of slip round the outer, and upper, edge of your base.

7. Using the rest of your long worm of clay, wind a coil over the layer of slip.

8. Cut this off an inch beyond the point at which you started, cutting through both layers of coil (Fig. 1c).

9. Remove the loose piece you have in the lower layer, and join the two ends together (Fig. 1d).

10. Put on another layer of slip, and add another coil, cutting and joining exactly the same as before, and continue until your pot is the right size. You can make some layers wider, gradually, or narrower and widen out again, to give an interesting shape.
11. When it is big enough, take your spatula and smooth over the outer or inner edge of the ridges, leaving the marks as they are making a pattern (Fig. 1e).
12. Decorate when dry, as with the first pot.

A Slab Pot

1. Roll out the clay with your hands, or a rolling-pin, so that you have an even slab of clay, about $\frac{1}{2}$ in. thick.
2. Cut out of this your base, and four sides (Fig. 2a).
3. With your finger put a thin layer of slip on the outer, upper edge of your base.
4. Put one side on to this (Fig. 2b).
5. Make a fillet of clay (this is a tiny sausage-shaped piece).
6. Place this along the inner, lower edge of your side where it joins on to the base (Fig. 2c).
7. With the spatula, work this gently into the join, to strengthen the pot.
8. Continue in the same way, adding the rest of the sides.
9. Dry and decorate as before.

All these models can be sent away to be fired, but before you embark on this idea you must ask the advice of a potter.

Cardboard Armour

You need scissors, pencil, cardboard, glue, paper, tape, paint and brushes.

A Shield

Take a piece of paper and fold it double. Draw on it one half of a shield and its crest. Cut round the drawing. Open the drawing and stick on to cardboard. Trim round the cardboard and paint the shield.

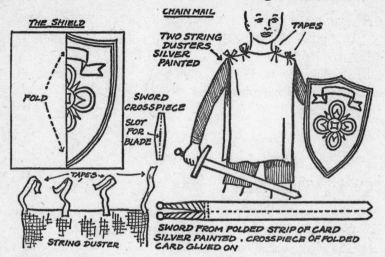

THE SHIELD

FOLD

CHAIN MAIL

TWO STRING DUSTERS SILVER PAINTED

TAPES

SWORD CROSSPIECE

SLOT FOR BLADE

TAPES

STRING DUSTER

SWORD FROM FOLDED STRIP OF CARD SILVER PAINTED. CROSSPIECE OF FOLDED CARD GLUED ON

Make a handle with a piece of tape as long as the widest part of the shield. Stick this at each side of the shield with 2-in. strips of adhesive tape.

A Sword
Draw a sword on cardboard (see diagram), cut it out, and paint it.

Chain Mail
You need two large string dusters, silver paint, tape, needle and cotton, old newspaper, paint-brush.

Lay the dusters on the newspaper on the floor. With a brush, paint over the dusters with silver paint. When dry, sew four tapes on to each duster, as in the drawing. To wear the chain mail, tie two tapes at each side of the neck and two on each shoulder.

A Tiny Top

Draw a circle round a penny on a piece of card. Cut it out, paint it, and put a spent matchstick you have sharpened to a point through the centre.

A Twizzler

Make a circle of stiff card. Make two holes in the middle and thread string through them. Swing card over and over to wind up, then tighten or slacken the string to make it spin.

Coconut Pyramids

You need 2 egg whites, 5 oz. caster sugar, 8 oz. desiccated coconut, cochineal or green colouring, baking sheet, rice paper.

1. Line a baking sheet with rice paper.
2. Whisk egg whites till very stiff. (To keep spare yolks, put them in a basin of cold water. They can be used later in scrambled eggs, see p. 54.)
3. Gradually add sugar and desiccated coconut to form a fairly stiff mixture.
4. Add two drops of colouring and stir well.
5. Arrange spoonsful on the tray and shape into cones.
6. Bake in a very cool oven at 250, regulo $\frac{1}{4}$, for 1–2 hours until pyramids are crisp. Do not let them brown.
7. Cool on a wire rack.

Chocolate Crispy Cakes

You need cornflakes or rice crispies, a bar of plain, milk or cooking chocolate, paper cases.

Put the chocolate in a basin and place it over a saucepan of hot water until it melts. Remove the basin and stir in the rice crispies or cornflakes, making sure to mix them so that they are all covered with chocolate.

Put a spoonful in each paper case and leave to set. In five minutes they will be ready to eat.

Games to Play

Silhouettes

You need a sheet of paper, 24 in. by 24 in. (black or white), soft pencil, table-lamp with a very bright bulb, scissors, drawing-pins or adhesive tape.

Seat the subject whose silhouette you wish to make on a chair close to the wall and fix the paper on the wall behind him with drawing-pins or adhesive tape.

Place the lamp so that the shadow of the sitter's head is thrown on to the paper. The brighter the light, the clearer the shadow will be.

Draw round the outline carefully with a soft pencil. Should you want a black silhouette use black paper. If you use white paper, mount it on black.

Newmarket

You need 2 packs of playing cards, and a supply of counters.

Newmarket can be played by two or more people. It is played with one pack of cards plus the ace of spades, king of diamonds, queen of hearts and jack of clubs from a second pack. These four cards are laid face upwards in the centre of the table and are known as 'horses'. The players all start with an agreed number of counters and before the cards are dealt each player places one or more counters on one of the four horses.

The aims of the game are (1) to have no cards left when the game is over and (2) the player holding one of the 'horses' in his hand must try to play it in order to win the counters on that card.

The cards are dealt to all the players, face downwards, plus one extra or dummy hand. The player on the left of the dealer starts the game by playing any card he likes, provided it is the lowest he has in a suit, for example the 2 of spades. He calls out the number and suit of the card, and places it on the table in front of him. The player having the 3 of spades must then play it, and so on until the sequence is played out – as there is a dummy hand, some of the cards will be in there. When play stops the last player either continues with the next card he has in that suit or starts on a fresh suit. As soon as one player has finished all his cards, the game is over and all the other players must pay him one counter for each remaining card in their hands. Any counters which have not been claimed from the horses must remain there until the next game.

Cherry-stone Jingles

These are games to play with the cherry or plum stones left on your plate. Say these jingles as you point to each stone:

> Tinker, Tailor, Soldier, Sailor, Rich Man,
> Poor Man, Beggarman, Thief.

or:

> Soldier brave, Sailor true,
> Skilled Physician, Oxford Blue,
> Learned Lawyer, Squire so hale,
> Dashing Airman, Curate pale.

Starting with the first stone again, say each of the following, repeating for all the stones:

> This year, next year, sometime, never,
> Coach, carriage, wheelbarrow, cart,
> Gold, silver, copper, brass,
> Silk, satin, cotton, rags,
> Boots, shoes, slipper, clogs,
> Church, chapel, cathedral, abbey,
> Big house, little house, pigsty, barn.

If you have for example, six stones on your plate, your story is this:

I will marry a Poor Man, or Squire so hale, next year, I will go in a Carriage made of Silver, wearing a Satin dress and Shoes, the wedding will be in a Chapel, and I will live in a Little House.

Tiddlywinks

One or more players, tiddlywinks, or buttons large and small, six egg-cups.

The object is to get as many tiddlywinks into the egg-cups as possible.

The easiest way to play is to place the cups in a row, line up small tiddlywinks opposite each cup, about two feet away, and see how many you can flip in. To do this you press the back of the small tiddlywink on the ground with the front edge of the larger one, held in your hand, and with practice you find you will be able to flip it into the cup.

You can play this as a competition, taking it in turns to see how many shots you take to get a 'wink in each cup.

If you have no tiddlywinks, use flat buttons, choosing a larger one as the presser.

Broken Bottles

Any number of people can play this ball game. They stand in a circle and throw the ball to each other, catching it with two hands. If a player drops the ball he must pay the following penalties:

First time – he uses his right hand only.
Second time – he uses his left hand only.
Third time – he kneels on one knee, but uses both hands.

Fourth time – he kneels on both knees, but uses both hands.
Fifth time – he kneels on both knees and uses right hand.
Sixth time – he kneels on both knees and uses left hand.
Seventh time: he is out.

Each time a player catches a ball while paying his penalties, he regains one place. For example – if a player has already dropped the ball twice running he has to catch the next ball with his left hand only. If he succeeds, he will catch the next one with his right hand, and if he succeeds again, he will catch the next ball with two hands.

For November Gardens

Outdoors

There is plenty of tidying up to do in the garden in November. The fallen leaves must be swept up and, if you live near a wood, it is a good idea to collect a sackful of leaf-mould. The best leaf-mould is found under oak and beech trees, and is used as required for digging into the garden or placing over plants to protect them during the winter.

Indoors: Apple, Peach and Plum Seeds

These seeds are not ready to plant as soon as they come out of the fruit. Put the seeds in a jar with damp moss and keep them in a refrigerator for about six weeks. Turn them over from time to time until they start to sprout. When this happens, plant them in the same way as orange and lemon pips (p. 43).

An aquarium planted with different kinds of tree saplings makes an attractive 'tree nursery'.

December

A Christmas Carol

The Darling of the world is come
And fit is it we find the room
To welcome Him. The nobler part
Of all the house here is the heart,
Which we will give Him; and bequeath
This holly and this ivy wreath
To do Him honour, who's our King
And Lord of all things revelling.

Robert Herrick

Christmas

By the beginning of December plum puddings are made, cards are being written, the holly is ready to be picked and the Christmas trees are waiting to be chosen.

Christmas is a time when families gather together and churches hold joyful services to celebrate that day when Jesus was born and the three kings, Caspar, Balthazar and Melchior brought Him gifts of gold, frankincense and myrrh. In memory of this we give each other presents.

The first Christmas trees date from the time of the German Apostle St Boniface, who replaced the sacred oak of the pagan god Odin with a fir tree, decorated and lighted with candles, in tribute to the baby Jesus. When Queen Victoria married Prince Albert of Saxe-Coburg-Gotha, he introduced this custom into England.

In early times it was usual to hang boxes in the churches for people to put in offerings for the poor and the needy. These were opened, and the money distributed, on the day after Christmas, which became known as Boxing Day.

The Robin

You will often see the robin this month, but that is not the real reason why it is the Christmas bird. Until about a hundred years ago, postmen wore red coats, and were nicknamed 'Robin', so when Christmas cards became popular the robin was used as a cheerful symbol of the postman.

Although the robin is very friendly to man, its nature is aggressive. In the spring when the cock's breast is a bright red it lays claim to a certain part of the garden or countryside and will defend it with the greatest boldness. In the winter the female robin claims a territory too and sings to defend it. She has a red breast but paler than the cock's. She lays four to six eggs, buff or mottled-beige colour, in a nest made of dead leaves and moss and lined with hair. Robins have a charming song of many notes and twitters.

December Flower

Evergreens

It is traditional to decorate the house at Christmas with evergreens: holly, ivy and mistletoe. There is a saying that if the holly has lots of berries it will be a cold, hard, winter.

Holly has small, white flowers and scarlet, glossy berries,

which are brilliant in appearance but very poisonous. It has dense, prickly, dark green leaves.

Ivy twines itself up trees and through hedgerows, climbing by means of its roots which cling like tiny, small claws to other plants. It has two different kinds of leaves and small flowers full of honey. When used for decoration it looks delicate and pretty.

Mistletoe grows on fruit and forest trees but mainly on apple, oak and hawthorn trees. The berries are eaten by birds, who carry them to other trees, where the seeds attach themselves to the branches and, when they germinate, pierce the bark and live on the wood of the tree. It is easy to establish mistletoe on a tree by rubbing the berries, when they are ripe at the end of February, on the underneath of young, healthy branches. The berries are white and have a single seed. Mistletoe is supposed to be lucky.

Carol Singers

The gates of the walled cities and towns of the Middle Ages were guarded by watchmen who were called waits. One of their duties was to sound the hours by playing a note or a simple tune on a wind instrument like an oboe. As many of the waits were musicians they gradually came to form bands which played on special occasions.

Later on, when cities had police forces, there was no need for watchmen or waits. But one of their duties had been to play songs for the Christmas festival in the streets. This is why carol singers are sometimes called waits.

They still call at houses before Christmas, but mostly they are children collecting money either for themselves or some good cause.

Stick Insects

Stick insects are remarkable examples of animal camouflage. They look exactly like the twigs or leaves of their food plant. Their bodies are brown or grey-brown and stick-like, sometimes with projections like thorns, and even sometimes with greenish lumps looking like moss-covered twigs. They live in tropical or semi-tropical countries but can easily be reared here on ivy or privet leaves. They move and feed only at night. Males are rare, and may appear only once in many generations. The eggs seem to be dropped anywhere on the ground, and are enclosed in hard little capsules, with a lid through which the new insect crawls out.

Getting Ready for Christmas

Christmas Decorations

Christmas Log

You need one small log split in half (about 12 in. would be good), small candles, fir cones, acorns, plasticine, wheat ears, white paint, artificial snow, any other decorations.

Place a large piece of newspaper on the table. Choose a log with a nice thick bark and an interesting uneven surface. Paint round the bark carefully with white paint and then sprinkle with artificial snow while it is still wet. When this has dried, take some plasticine and roll into a thick 'worm'. Press this along the top of the log, and stick your holly leaves, candles and fir cones, wheat ears and acorns, all tipped with white paint and covered in artificial snow, into the plasticine.

Frozen Pond

You need a mirror, glue, artificial snow, cotton wool, toy figures and animals, fir cones, acorns and beech nut husks.

Lay a mirror flat on a large piece of newspaper on a table. Put a thin layer of glue round the outside edge of the mirror, and stick cotton wool on to this so that the edge is hidden. Fluff the cotton wool to make it uneven (this makes the border and snow-covered hedge round your pond). If you like the idea you can put a thin streak of glue across the mirror from corner to corner and on to this also stick cotton wool, to form a line of snow across the middle of the pond. On the glass arrange some little figures. Father Christmas, a bear, some birds, and small dogs who will be reflected in the mirror as if they are skating. Stick fir cones, acorns, or beech-nut husks, painted white, into the cotton wool for tiny trees, and sprinkle with artificial snow.

Tying a Parcel

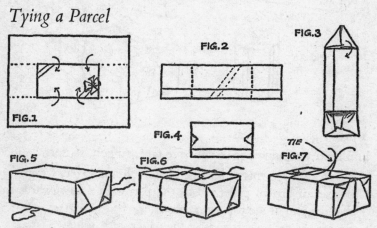

1. Lay the paper flat on a table or on the floor.
2. Place the article to be wrapped in the centre of the paper (Fig. 1).
3. Fold the two long edges over the top of the article (Fig. 2) and neatly turn in the ends to form a point (Fig. 3). Fold these flaps over the top of the parcel (Fig. 4). Turn the parcel over to stop these flaps from unwrapping.
4. Take a piece of string and fold it in half. Lay it on the table and place the parcel on top of it (Fig. 5).
5. Slip the two ends of the string through the loop and round the edge of the parcel (Fig. 6).

6. Turn the parcel over and loop the ends of the string through the cross strings on the other side (Fig. 7).
7. Tie the ends in a firm knot and cut off any lengths of string which are left over.

Wrapping Christmas Presents

FIG.1　　FIG.2a

FIG.2b

A pretty parcel is a pleasure.

You need wrapping paper, adhesive tape, ribbon, scissors.

1. Wrap your presents as described before, but use a gay wrapping instead of brown paper. Place the parcel face downwards so that the join of the paper is at the back.
2. Secure the centre and ends of the paper with adhesive tape.
3. Tie the parcel as described previously, using ribbon instead of string, and finishing off with a bow instead of a knot. An easy way is to tie one length of ribbon round the widest part of the parcel (Fig. 1).
4. To tie a larger oblong, square, or round parcel use a four-way ribbon. Pass the centre of the ribbon under the front of the parcel, which should still be face down, bring up the ends and cross them across the bottom (Fig. 2a). Holding the ends of the ribbon carefully, turn the parcel over so that it is the right way up. Pass the ends round the centre ribbon and tie in a firm

double knot. Now arrange a bow in the centre, making sure that the ends and the bows are the same length (Fig. 2b).

5. A more ambitious tie is a diagonal one. Start with the parcel the right way up this time. With a long piece of ribbon take the long end from D and under the corner A, as shown in the drawing. Pass this end over the front, and under corner C. Tie near corner D.

A Box to Put Presents In

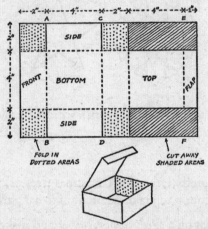

You can make it any size you need provided the card you use is in the same proportions. To make one 4 in. square use a piece of card 8 in. wide by 13 in. long. You will also need ruler, pencil, scissors, glue.

1. Rule off the card into 2-in. squares, leaving a 1-in. strip at one end (see above).
2. Fold along dotted lines.
3. Cut down the thick lines.
4. Cut out diagonally shaded part on diagram.
5. Fold up end AB, putting the dotted corners towards the inside.
6. Fold up on line CD, putting in dotted corners as above.

7. Glue sides together, seeing that the long side is on the outer edge.

8. Crease over the 1 in. strip at EF for flap, and tuck in at the front of the box. Paint or decorate.

Milk Top Decorations

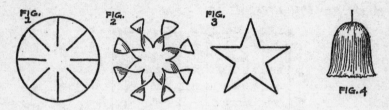

You need bottle tops (not split or torn), scissors, needle and cotton, ball-point pen.

A Flower

These are very pretty either for Christmas trees or, with father's help, strung on cotton to make decorations to hang from the light.

1. Put the top flat on a sheet of newspaper and make four cuts of about ½ in. long, dividing it into quarters. Now make four other equal cuts (Fig. 1).

2. Holding the top in the centre with finger and thumb, twist each wing sideways (Fig. 2).

3. With a needle, draw a thread of cotton through the centre and tie it into a loop.

Stars

1. With a ball-point pen draw a star on the inside of the top (Fig. 3).

2. Cut out and thread cotton through the top of the star.

Bells

1. Very carefully press out the edges, and put the milk top over your first finger.
2. Mould the top down and press out folds, taking care not to make any sharp points or you might cut your fingers.
3. Shape the bottom into a round (Fig. 4).
4. To hang, knot the end of a piece of cotton and thread with a needle.

An Advent Calendar

In Scandinavian countries Advent is always an important time and the children make calendars to mark the time from Advent Sunday, at the beginning of December, until Christmas Day. It is easy to make one of these and exciting to open a window each day.

To make the calendar you need two pieces of stiff black paper 12 in. by 16 in., scissors, glue, ribbon, old Christmas cards. There are diagrams on the next page.

1. On one sheet of paper draw 25 windows, 24 the same size and one large one for Christmas Day (Fig. 1).
2. Cut these windows carefully with scissors so that they can be shut and opened (Fig. 2).
3. Turn the paper on to the wrong side and paste all around the edge being very careful not to use too much glue and not to get any on the backs of the windows.
4. Put this sheet on the second piece of paper and press under a heavy weight until the glue is quite dry.
5. Paste a small picture into each window. Try to choose pictures connected with Christmas or winter. Cut them out very carefully and place them in the centre of each window (Fig. 3).
6. Close all the windows and write the date under them in white ink, starting with 1 December and finishing on the 25.
7. Finally, make two holes in the centre of the top of your calendar and thread a ribbon through to hang it up.

December Indoors

Another way to make your calendar is shown in Fig. 4.

1. Cut out two circles of paper and make the windows round the edge like the numbers on a clock.
2. Cut out a stiff cardboard hand and stick it through the middle of the calendar with a split paper-clip and turn the hand on to a new window each day, as you open them.

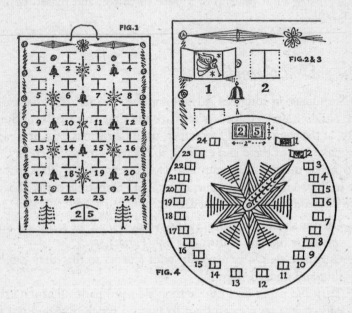

Puppet Theatre

You need glue, some ¼-in. balsa, balsa cement, piano wire, eleven old cereal packets, old photographs, card and cardboard, newspaper, flour paste.

For the Theatre

1. Take six cereal packets the same size and stick down all the flaps. Glue two packets together side by side (Fig. 1). Glue another two packets together and then the final two packets. Allow to dry.

2. Glue the three pairs together end to end (Fig. 2) and cover with newspaper stuck on with flour paste.

3. Take two more cereal packets and stick the bottom of each box on to the top of the front of this stage, one at each end. Stick the three remaining boxes end to end and, when they have dried, stick them across the top of the stage (Fig. 3). To

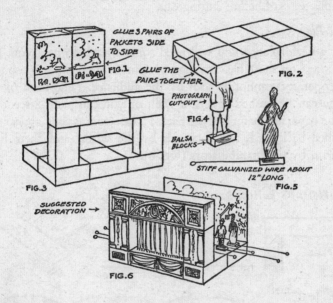

finish off the front of the stage cover it with newspaper stuck on with flour paste, as for the floor. When dry, paint with poster colours. If you wish, you can paint a curtain on some card (Fig. 6).

The Actors

1. Find some old photographs or pictures of people and carefully cut out, leaving ¼ in. on the bottom of each one.

2. Cut two pieces of ¼-in.-square balsa about 1½ in. long.

3. Stick one on to the front and one on to the back of the piece left at the bottom of the actor (Fig. 4).

4. Take a piece of wire about 18 in. long and make a loop in one end.
5. Push the other end into the end of the balsa wood and stick (Fig. 5).

Make as many actors as you wish in this way and put them on one side ready for your first play. You may have to stick the photographs on card before cutting out.

The Play

For a performance you will need some friends to help you. Put the stage on the table. Arrange curtains around the stage so that the operators cannot be seen by the audience. (The back of the stage can be pushed against a wall, or you can paint a scene on some paper and hang it at the back.) The actors as they appear are pushed backwards and forwards by the wires, and their lines spoken by the manipulators (Fig. 6).

Christmas Chains

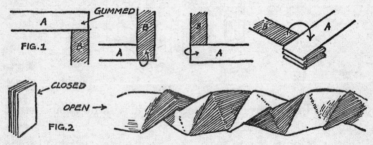

You need long strips of paper 1–2 in. wide, glue.

1. Place two strips of paper at right angles to each other and glue one corner on top of the other (Fig. 1).
2. Fold lower strip over upper, left over right, top over bottom, right over left (Fig. 2), and continue these movements. Loosen to see if the chain is long enough. To join in another strip, glue the end carefully on top of the old strip, and in the same direction.

Presents Made from Felt

Felt is a good idea for quick presents because it comes in lovely colours, is thick, and the edges don't fray, so you have much less sewing to do. But it doesn't wash well, so you must keep it very clean while you are working with it. (Diagrams on next page.)

A Pencil Case
1. Cut a strip of felt 3½ in. wide and 3 in. longer than a new pencil.
2. Cut another strip the same width, but 1 in. shorter than the pencil.
3. Sew the two sides and the bottom of the case together on the right side, using a running stitch or a blanket stitch. It looks nice if you use a thick, coloured embroidery silk.
4. Mark three lines with a ruler to divide the case into four compartments and stitch down these lines, using running stitch, again in a bright colour. Be very careful to keep the lines straight. Make a loop on the top and either sew a button to the front, or sew on a press stud to fasten the case (Fig. 1).

A Felt Bookmark
This is a useful way of using up scraps of felt.
1. Cut a strip of felt 9 in. by 1½ in. and cut a fringe each end.
2. Embroider the bookmark in coloured silks. Remember that the back will show when the pages are turned over, so keep it tidy (Fig. 2).

A Comb Case
1. Cut two strips of felt 7 in. by 2 in., or according to the size of comb you have.
2. Embroider on one piece, then join the two pieces round three sides with blanket or running stitch (Fig. 3).

A Needle Case
1. Cut three strips of felt 6 in. by 3 in., two of one colour for the needles and one different colour for the cover.

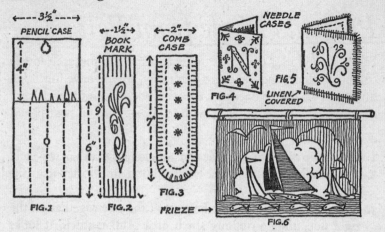

PENCIL CASE
BOOK MARK
COMB CASE
NEEDLE CASES
FIG.4
FIG.5
LINEN-COVERED
FIG.1
FIG.2
FIG.3
FRIEZE
FIG.6

2. Stitch the three together in the centre and fold. If you can, cut the edges of the inner pieces with pinking shears, to make it prettier.

3. Embroider on the cover and press with a warm iron when you have finished (Fig. 4). You could use plain linen for the cover, pull threads out around the edge and embroider the centre (Fig. 5).

A Felt Frieze or Picture (for older children)

You need hessian or linen, felt, scissors, glue, embroidery silk and needle, warm iron, bamboo pole.

1. Take a piece of hessian or embroidery linen, twice the length your picture is to be.

2. Fold it in half with the right sides together and stitch the two long sides together.

3. Turn to the right side, sew up the remaining sides, iron.

4. Cut felt shapes to make your picture. Trace paper patterns for this from books, if you like. Arrange them, glue on and, when dry, embroider detail.

5. Stick or sew three ribbon loops on to the top. Thread a bamboo pole through to hang the picture (Fig. 6).

Fudge

You need 4 oz. margarine, 1 lb. sugar, 2 large dessertspoonfuls golden syrup, 6 large dessertspoonfuls condensed milk, thick saucepan, shallow baking tin.

Grease the baking tin. Melt the margarine in a thick saucepan over a low heat. Blend in the syrup and the sugar and bring them slowly to the boil, stirring occasionally. Add the condensed milk, stirring all the time. Boil until a little of the mixture, dropped into cold water, forms a firm ball. Remove from the heat and keep stirring until the fudge is a stiff creamy mixture, then pour into a greased pan. Run a knife across it to make slices before it is quite cold. When it *is* cold always put it on to greaseproof paper.

You can flavour this mixture with coffee, melted chocolate, chopped nuts or raisins. Be sure and make enough, because *everybody* likes it.

December Gardening

Flowers for Christmas

You can start preparing leaves and dried flowers for Christmas decorations quite early in the month. Earlier in the year you will have dried corn, wheat, bracken, hydrangea and poppy heads. Now you can get sprays of holly and one or two twigs to add to them. On the twigs, which can be about 18 in. high, hang silver baubles, tinsel and other tree decorations.

The twigs can be made to stand up in plasticine (1 in. deep and 2 in. across) which has been pressed on to the middle of a silver cardboard cake base.

Shoe whitener or gold and silver paint can be used for painting leaves and twigs.

Games to Play

What's the Time, Mr Wolf?

This is a variation of 'He'. One player is chosen as Mr Wolf, then he walks away, to be followed by the other children asking 'What's the time, Mr Wolf?' He then replies with any time he likes: one, two, three o'clock, and so on. When Mr Wolf replies 'Twelve o'clock, dinner time' the followers have to run for home before being caught. The last one home, or the one caught, is the next Mr Wolf.

Charades

This is the very best game for family parties, because most grown-ups enjoy it as much as you do. You don't even have to dress up, but it's more fun if you do, so it's a good idea to have a selection of odd hats, coats, scarves, sheets, dressing gowns, etc., all together in the room where you make your plans. Sometimes the clothes will suggest a word. But, in case you are all too excited to think clearly, it's a good idea to have a list of words to fall back on. Two-syllable words are enough for younger players.

Here are some words which work well and are easy to act: carrot, bargain, earwig, kidnap, partridge, knapsack, bandage and carpet. It will make the charade more difficult if you choose two words and act them both at the same time in order to confuse the audience.

The Rules

Divide the players into two teams, A and B: four each is a good number. Draw lots to see which team will act first and that team then leaves the room. The team must choose a word of two or three syllables like one of the examples above. Each syllable must be acted in a separate scene and then finally the whole word together. For example, *car*, then *pet*, and finally *carpet*. Team B must then try to guess the chosen word. Even if they do not guess the right answer they should have the next turn.

Mime Game

The players act a saying or a nursery rhyme, but it must be in dumb show or you will give the game away too quickly. Here are a few which could be acted:

'Too many cooks spoil the broth.'
'You can lead a horse to the water, but you cannot make him drink.'
'Many hands make light work.'
'It's an ill wind that blows nobody any good.'
'All work and no play makes Jack a dull boy.'
'An apple a day keeps the doctor away.'
'Little Miss Muffet sat on a tuffet.'
'Little Jack Horner sat in a corner.'
'Ride a cock horse to Banbury Cross.'

Index

Index